CANAL WALKS

NORTH

RAY QUINLAN

ALAN SUTTON

To Hattie *who else?*

First published in the United Kingdom in 1993 by
Alan Sutton Publishing Ltd · Phoenix Mill · Stroud · Gloucestershire

British Library Cataloguing in Publication Data

Quinlan, Ray
  Canal Walks: North
  I. Title
  914.204

    ISBN 0-86299-995-2

Library of Congress Cataloging in Publication Data applied for

Typeset in 10/12 Plantin.
Typesetting and origination by
Alan Sutton Publishing Limited.
Printed and bound in Great Britain by
WBC, Bridgend, Mid Glam.

KEY TO MAPS

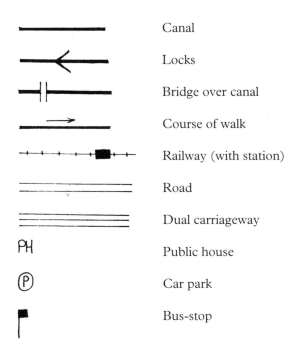

Canal

Locks

Bridge over canal

Course of walk

Railway (with station)

Road

Dual carriageway

Public house

Car park

Bus-stop

LOCATION OF WALKS

1. Aire & Calder Navigation at Knottingley
2. Bridgewater Canal at Worsley
3. Chesterfield Canal at Worksop
4. Fossdyke Navigation at Lincoln
5. Huddersfield Canals at Huddersfield
6. Lancaster Canal at Glasson Dock
7. Leeds & Liverpool Canal at Skipton
8. Macclesfield Canal at Macclesfield
9. Peak Forest Canal at Whaley Bridge
10. Ripon Canal at Ripon
11. Rochdale Canal at Hebden Bridge
12. Sankey Brook Navigation at Widnes

ACKNOWLEDGEMENTS

This book would have been impossible without the splendid resources of various libraries: communal ownership in practice. Despite chronic under-funding, the information and help received was substantial.

Help and advice came from many of the local societies and trusts viz.: Dave Edmunds and Pat Jones of the Ripon Motor Boat Club, Richard Willis of the Ripon Canal Society, the Sankey Canal Restoration Society, the Lancaster Canal Trust and the Macclesfield Canal Society. Thanks also to the various employees of British Waterways who, as ever, have been both helpful and co-operative.

Assistance with archive photographs came from Lynn Doylerush of the Boat Museum and Sue Furness of the College of Ripon and York St John. Assistance with, though no responsibility for, the author's pictures came from Mr Ilford and Mr Fuji and two, old and steadily disintegrating, Olympuses fitted with 28 mm and 75–150 mm lenses.

For rest and recuperation during walking trips, thanks go to David and Dorothy in Blackburn and Nigel and Rachel in Mirfield. As before, much appreciation to Taffy for most of the transportation. And, of course, thanks to Mary who continued to provide her wonderful support throughout.

CONTENTS

INTRODUCTION

In the early planning of this series of three books, I had the feeling that the canals of England were a largely undiscovered resource. I was wrong. It was just that they were a largely unrecognized one.

It's been a year and a half of gestation and nearly 600 miles along forty-six different canals and navigations. Virtually everywhere, I've been amazed at the numbers of people who enjoy our waterways without ever getting into a boat or ever plonking themselves down on the bank armed to the teeth with hook, line and simmering cauldron of maggots. Admittedly there have been times when I've felt completely alone. There are some almost eerie stretches of the Kennet & Avon through Wiltshire, some undeniably deserted sections of the Grantham, and I've never felt as lonely as on the Birmingham Canal in Smethwick. But in other places the canals have become positive tourist attractions. Anyone who has been to the Foxton Locks or to Stoke Bruerne will testify to this. These are the places where day-trippers simply go for a gentle amble along a cultured towpath or for a philosophical stare into the whirling eddies of escaping lock water. Then there are the hiker routes over rougher ground. Here you'll find folk like me with our rucksacks and walking boots. We, identifiable as people who tuck our trousers into our socks, head off into the distance like well-orientated bees even if the driving rain has already seeped into our misnamed water-proofs. The prime sites for us are lines like the three cross-Pennine routes described in this volume.

But those canals are the obvious attractions; the ones where I would have expected to see people. The surprise came in the popularity of the less spectacular and the less well known. These are the waterways which hold no significant attraction, offer no particular 'sight to see', do not present the long-distance challenge but which are still popular for local folk walking the local dog. These are the places for a gentle jog, a brief saunter or an afternoon picnic. You'll see plenty of families out for a Sunday stroll along the Leeds & Liverpool or the Thames & Severn. Seemingly miles from any-where on the Bridgwater & Taunton you'll find an old lady walking the pet mongrel. Under the big sky on Romney Marsh, you'll come across a couple of kids bird watching along the Royal Military. On the towpath of the Sankey Brook Navigation, in the shadow of the massive Fiddlers Ferry power station, you'll pass a pair of mums wheeling a pair of pushchairs with a pair of toddlers admiring the view. I think I said hello to more people in half an hour along the Worcester & Birmingham than in a whole day in the centre of Brum itself. And even by the long-abandoned lengths of canal – such as the Chesterfield above Worksop – you'll find them. Just ambling. Just looking. Just enjoying.

The nation was there before me! The towpaths of the once-derelict and ignored canals are now as popular a place for a walk as anywhere in the country. And yet they are still not recognized as the great national resource that they are. Only a minor proportion of the towpaths of England are designated public rights of way. British Waterways, who let's face it do a pretty good job on our behalf, retain the right to close the non-designated paths at will. Fine now, when the political mood is in the public's favour, but who's to say where and when things may change.

The Inland Waterways Association and the Towpath Action Group have been campaigning for some years that, where possible, towpaths are declared public rights of way and that the genuine rights of access be maintained. We, the people who enjoy these wonderful legacies, should support them in their crusade and, in the mean time, simply keep making the most of it.

The Northern Canals

The northern canals are full of contrast. There's the quiet rural routes of the Chesterfield, the Fossdyke, the Lancaster, vast stretches of the Leeds & Liverpool, the Macclesfield and the Ripon. There's the cross-Pennine journeys up the old mill valleys with the Rochdale and the Huddersfield. There's the busy country around the Peak Forest. Then there's derelict or inner-city sections of canals like the Bridgewater and the Sankey Brook. On top of all that, there's the only 'canal' covered in this series that is still used for the purpose for which it was designed: the Aire & Calder Navigation.

And it's all good walking territory.

Of course, this is just a selection of the canals of the north and although by no means arbitrary, it is strictly a personal choice. Walkers should not ignore the Pocklington or the Market Weighton in Yorkshire. Just south of Manchester there's the Ashton. We never even get near the Sheffield & South Yorkshire or the Stainforth & Keadby. We only scratch the surface of the Calder & Hebble. And then what about the long-lost canals such as the Carlisle, the Barnsley and the Manchester, Bolton & Bury? All these are worthy of further investigation and, with the aid of an Ordnance Survey map and some keen legs, they can be traced both on paper and, often, on the ground.

As with all personal choices, some people's favourite lines or stretches of waterway may have been omitted. There is also the problem of what is a northern canal. The Trent & Mersey Canal certainly goes as far north as the Macclesfield even though the former was included in *Canal Walks: Midlands.* In all these matters, only the author is to blame. I have not tried to be a sage on these matters, merely a stimulus. Walking the canals of the north should be an adventure with plenty to see and to discover for yourselves. And it is quite likely that you will see even more than I did and enjoy them every bit as much.

Walking the Towpaths

The walks in this book are all straightforward and require no special feats of strength or navigation. Towpath walks have two great virtues: they are mostly on the flat and they have a ready-made, unmistakable course to follow. Getting lost should therefore, in theory at least, be relatively hard. The key problem with towpath walks is that if you want to spend most of the day by the canal, circular routes to and from a vehicle or a particular station or bus-stop become difficult. Many of the walks in this volume involve walking one way and returning by public transport. This means that you must check the availability of the bus or train before travelling. Telephone numbers are provided and your local library should have the main British Rail timetable.

Walkers should generally plan for 2 to 2¹/₂ miles an hour so that stops can be made for sightseeing or a break. Head-down speedsters should easily manage three miles an hour on a good track. You should, of course, add a little time for stoppages for refreshment and add a lot of time if you are accompanied by photographers or bird watchers.

No special equipment or provisions are needed to walk the towpaths of England. On a good day and on a good path any comfortable footwear and clothing will do, and you'll be able to leave the laden rucksack at home. However, for longer walks through more remote country you should be more prudent. Even in a drought, towpaths can be extremely muddy and, from experience, it can not only rain virtually any time but usually does. Boots and a raincoat of some sort are therefore advisable. Similarly, although pubs and small shops are often fairly common along the way, it may be useful to carry some kind of snack and drink with you.

This book includes sketch maps that show the route to be taken. However, the local Ordnance Survey map will always be useful and the appropriate map numbers and references are provided in each chapter. Again your local library may well have them for loan.

Finally, the dangers inherent in walking along a waterway are often not fully appreciated. Over the 1990 Christmas holiday, three children died after falling into a lock on the Kennet & Avon at Burghfield. A year later their mother committed suicide having been unable to endure her loss. Locks are deep, often have silt-laden bottoms, and are very difficult to get out of. Everybody, especially children, should be made aware of this. If somebody does fall in, you should not go into the water except as a last resort. You should LIE on the bank and use something like a coat for the person to grab so that you can then pull them out. Better still, keep children away from the edge.

Otherwise, please enjoy.

1
THE AIRE & CALDER NAVIGATION

Knottingley

Introduction

The A&CN is one of the nation's most successful commercial waterways and, unlike most of the network, is thriving and producing a profit even to this day. That novel fact alone should make it worth a visit.

The River Calder has its source in the Pennines north of Todmorden. It becomes the Aire & Calder Navigation at Wakefield from where the line passes via Stanley to Castleford. The source of the River Aire is in Malham Tarn. It becomes the Aire & Calder Navigation at Leeds from where it goes south-east via Woodlesford to Castleford. The combined waters now head east to Knottingley where the navigation splits. A northern branch follows the River Aire to Haddlesey and then the Selby Canal to Selby and the River Ouse. The southern branch, a cut called the Knottingley & Goole Canal, takes traffic to the Ouse at Goole.

For those who like their canals to be narrow, winding, overhung by trees and full of pretty holiday narrow boats, the A&CN will come as a bit of a shock. But it's worth walking just to see what a modern waterway is really like and it is certainly far from uninteresting.

History

From the Middle Ages, the woollen products of Leeds and Wakefield had been exported overland to York and Selby on the River Ouse or to Knottingley on the River Aire for subsequent shipment to Europe. The Aire had been navigable from Airmyn on the Ouse as far as Knottingley since medieval times but the towns to the west needed an improved transport network if they were to compete and grow. As a result, the seventeenth century saw several attempts to extend the waterway along both the Rivers Aire and Calder. A series of bills were presented to Parliament (in 1621, 1625 and 1679) and were defeated, mostly through the objection of the city of York who feared loss of trade.

By 1690 some 2,000 tons of goods p.a. were being moved from the towns of the West Riding by cart at a cost of almost £3 a ton. The merchants of Leeds and Wakefield were thus becoming increasingly convinced of the necessity of a navigable waterway and the scheme was revived. Apart from the export of cloth, the new navigation would facilitate the import of wool and allow greater exploitation of west Yorkshire coal. John Hadley was asked to survey the Aire, and Samuel Shelton to survey the Calder. York Corporation once again objected claiming that it would drain the Ouse. However, Trinity House, in an independent report, disagreed and the A&CN Act received its Royal Assent on 4 May 1699.

The ownership of the navigation was vested in trustees who acted on behalf of the subscribers. These then divided themselves into a Leeds Committee and a Wakefield Committee. John Hadley was engaged as engineer and work started. The plan was to use the natural course of the rivers where possible and to only build new cuts where absolutely necessary. One major exception to this was the Crier Cut near Woodlesford which bypassed a highly convoluted section of the Aire towards Leeds. The work appears to have progressed smoothly and the first boats to navigate from the Ouse reached Leeds on 20 November 1700. The line to Wakefield was completed in 1701. Over the next few years, a series of improvements were also made to the Aire below Knottingley. This included the construction of locks at Beal and Haddlesey in order to raise the water levels along the line. By 1704 the navigation was fully operational. It consisted of sixteen locks (each about 60 ft by 15 ft) and had cost approximately £26,700.

The navigation was worked by contracting the line to lessees who paid a fee to the shareholders, as well as for any outgoings and repairs. In 1704 the annual rent was £800; by 1729 it had risen to £2,600 p.a. at a time when the freight and toll receipts were averaging around £6,000 annually. This meant that the undertakers were already receiving dividends of between 6 and 12 per cent. The traffic at this time was primarily in woollen goods exported from Leeds, Wakefield, Halifax and Bradford. Wool and corn were imported, mainly from Lincolnshire and East Anglia. There was also a healthy trade in coal from Wakefield to the Humber and then along the Ouse to York. Boats took 3–4 days to travel upstream from Airmyn to Leeds or Wakefield and 2–3 days back.

By the 1750s receipts were more than £9,000 p.a., Rawcliffe and Airmyn were developing as navigation centres, and the company was gradually ridding itself of confrontations with the river's millers by simply buying them out. In 1758 Sir Henry Ibbotson and Peter Birt took over the lease which now stood at £6,000 p.a., equivalent to a dividend of 20 per cent. By this time there was a regular coasting service from Airmyn to London and trade continued to rise. About three-quarters of the traffic was in coal, limestone, lime and manure, although the import of wool and the export of cloth remained a significant trade. With the arrival of the canal age, a range of connecting lines was proposed and built. Navigation along the River Calder had been extended towards Halifax and was opened to Sowerby Bridge in 1774. Beyond this, a wholly new cut, the Rochdale Canal, promised a waterway to Manchester. A canal Act passed in May 1770 enabled a new line from the A&CN at Leeds to Liverpool. All three routes would use the A&CN to Hull.

By now the old A&CN was beginning to look rather dated. Many of the lock sills were very shallow and shoals were common during summer months. In an attempt to placate complaints, the undertakers called in John Smeaton to recommend improvements. The objective was to produce a line able to take craft carrying 30–45 tons all year round. His recommendations, published in January 1772, included dredging, rebuilding locks and making a number of new cuts. The suggested cuts included a bypass canal from above Haddlesey Lock on the south side of the river to Gowdall above Snaith with two locks. A second bypass was to run from Brotherton (just below Knottingley). Other new cuts were proposed at Leeds, Knostrop, Woodlesford and Methley. Smeaton also recommended that the undertakers obtain powers to remove obstructions and to build a towpath.

The users of the navigation weren't satisfied with this and demanded more improvements. Such was the demand that rival schemes arose which would have bypassed the A&CN altogether. The Went Canal was to run from Wakefield to the Dutch River at Went Mouth. The Leeds & Selby Canal was to run from Leeds to the Ouse at Selby. However, the A&CN revised its own plans to include new cuts from Ferrybridge to above Beal, a series of bypass cuts from Leeds to Castleford and, perhaps most significantly, a line from Haddlesey to Selby (the Selby Canal). In the event, the rival schemes were defeated by effective lobbying from the A&CN while its own plans were passed. The new cuts (excluding the Woodlesford which wasn't built) were engineered by William Jessop with the Pinkerton brothers as contractors. The line to Selby was opened on 24 April 1778. Apart from improving the route to Hull, it significantly shortened the distance from the Wakefield collieries to York.

The various improvements had cost approximately £60,000 but the prudence of the investment is shown by the fact that toll receipts rose from an average of £22,857 p.a. in 1779–81 to £43,376 in 1791–3. Coal was the single largest cargo although there was a vigorous trade in corn, stone, lime, cloth bales, wool and groceries. The Selby line was such a success that the

A&CN's offices and yards at Airmyn were closed and a new centre opened in Selby. By 1792 trade was so brisk that further improvements could be made. Selby and Castleford Locks were altered and there was a new cut at Cross Channel. The navigation was able to support the promotion of the Barnsley Canal (from near Wakefield to that town) and a line south from the Barnsley to the River Don at Swinton (the Dearne & Dove Canal). There was also a general upgrading of all locks so that boats of 18 ft beam could work the line.

By 1805 prospects must have looked very good with the Rochdale route to Manchester completed and the Huddersfield and Leeds & Liverpool lines due to open. By the time the latter was finished in 1816, the annual toll income had risen to over £70,000. The confidence that this instilled meant that in 1818 the undertakers could propose a wholly new line from the A&CN at Haddlesey to the Dutch River at Newbridge, just six miles from Goole. The new cut would bypass the much convoluted and shoaled lower Aire and thus improve the route to Hull and the River Trent. Rival promotions were in the wind and the A&CN was already feeling the competition from other inland waterways following the opening of the Grand Junction Canal to London. John Rennie, reporting in January 1819, altered the course of the new line to run from Knottingley to Newbridge and then parallel to the Dutch River. He estimated the cost at £137,700. The enabling Act, passed in 1820, also allowed the A&CN to reorganize so that it now had a Board of Directors (although it was still not incorporated).

Several revisions were subsequently made to the plan. The junction with the A&CN was moved upstream to Ferrybridge rather than Knottingley. The line was deepened to take vessels carrying 100 tons. There was also to be a new barge basin and ship dock at Goole so that transhipment would occur there rather than at Hull. Following the death of John Rennie in 1822, George Leather was appointed engineer and to oversee further improvements along both the Aire and the Calder including the widening of more locks to the 18 ft beam. The first commercial vessel to pass along the new Knottingley & Goole Canal did so on 20 July 1826. The new line was 18½ miles long and could be travelled by fly-boat in just three hours. The Goole ship lock was able to handle vessels of 300–400 tons and the dock to which it led measured 600 ft by 200 ft and was 17 ft deep. Alongside these was a barge dock and lock. Ship and barge docks were linked by a short cut as well as a tramway. With the new docks at Goole, the cost had spiralled to £361,484, most of which had to be borrowed. In 1827 Goole was officially designated as a port, and custom facilities were set up.

Meanwhile Leather recommended that the rest of the line be made to a depth of 7 ft to allow the passage of boats carrying 100 tons. Sir John Rennie (junior) recommended a new cut below Wakefield to short cut the meandering line to Castleford. There were also plans to upgrade the River

Aire into what, in effect, was a Ferrybridge to Leeds Canal. But the A&CN hesitated, saying that the Goole Canal had exhausted its funds. This hesitation allowed in further rival plans. One group, headed by Thomas Lee and Shepley Watson, ran for 12 miles along the north side of the Calder from Wakefield to Ferrybridge. Only after the A&CN had pledged to improve the Calder was this plan defeated in Parliament and only then by just three votes. The A&CN employed Thomas Telford to review the state of the Calder above Ferrybridge. He proposed a cut from a point above Kirkthorpe Lock to cross the river via an aqueduct at Stanley Ferry to run to Fairies Hill (south of Methley) where three new cuts would further shorten the route to Castleford. Although Lee and Watson reworked their scheme, it was again defeated in Parliament and the A&CN's own plan received Royal Assent in June 1828. These improvements were estimated to cost £313,570 and an expansion of the Goole Docks added a further £148,850.

The 1830s saw a period of innovation. Steam packets had been used for several years, but in 1831 the company started to employ steam tugs to pull fly-boats on the Leeds to Goole run. The packet-boats between Goole and Castleford could average 6–7 miles per hour. In 1835 there were even two paddle-steamers, each able to carry 100 people, plying the line to Leeds. By April 1835 the continuous line of 7 ft depth from Leeds to Castleford was opened. The Calder Cut didn't open until August 1839 but the new line at 7½ miles was 5 miles shorter than the river route. The cost of the works increased the A&CN's debt in 1835 to £341,100. Repaying it had enforced a reduction in the funds allocated to dividends from £70,000 p.a. in the mid-1820s to, a still extremely healthy, £54,000 throughout the 1830s.

The threat of railway competition was first raised in 1824 when the Leeds & Hull Rail Road Company was proposed. The threat didn't materialize, however, until 22 September 1834 when the Leeds & Selby Railway opened. By now the A&CN was a powerful outfit. Tolls were cut by 40 per cent on 1 October 1834 (goods traffic along the railway was due to begin on 15 December), and by September 1836 it was the railway company that was seeking agreement on keeping the tolls up. The A&CN refused as its income had been only slightly reduced during what could have been a difficult period. In fact, by 1838, toll revenue was higher than it was in 1834. Only when the Selby railway was extended to Hull on 1 July 1840 did the A&CN's revenue begin to fall. From £145,511 in 1840, income was down to £114,654 just five years later. With great rapidity, new railways were opened to provide lines from Leeds and Selby to York, as well as connections to London and the south. In October 1841 the A&CN met with the Calder & Hebble Navigation and the Rochdale Canal with a view to fighting the onslaught. A common pricing policy and a general reduction in tolls was agreed in principle but not in practice. The potential for a concerted effort thus collapsed. In 1845 the Wakefield, Pontefract & Goole Railway (later to merge with the Manchester & Leeds to become the Lancashire & Yorkshire) was authorized, and by 1 April 1848 the line was carrying coal and the A&CN was unable to compete for passenger traffic. While a lot of the business attracted to rail was new, the navigation was still forced to compete by lowering tolls with a consequently reduced income. The main trade along the line by this time was in corn from Lincolnshire being shipped to the West Riding, with coal as a back carriage. There was, however, some measure of agreement between the old navigation and the new railway. At Goole the A&CN spent over £77,000 on new railway docks for which the L&Y paid a rent. In 1855 attempts to produce an agreement with the L&Y and North-Eastern Railways failed and the A&CN found itself in an even fiercer price war. Reductions in tolls had to be made. Receipts which stood at just over £108,854 in 1846 were down to £66,115 in 1856. Agreement was reached during the latter half of 1856 and tolls were raised once again.

In 1855 the Rochdale Canal was leased by four railway companies who promptly raised toll rates as a way of moving traffic onto rail. With increasing competition on its own route, it wasn't too long before the A&CN became receptive to a similar proposal. In 1856 the L&Y and the North-Eastern proposed a 21 year lease in return for £45,000 p.a. as a dividend plus the 4 per cent interest on the outstanding debt of £420,000. The agreement would include an option to apply for an amalgamation Act. However, the shareholders were against this and by 1858 the scheme was dropped.

The A&CN committee now changed philosophy and became determined to keep control of both its own and its neighbouring lines. Feeling that it could better maintain traffic by controlling the Calder & Hebble, it agreed with that navigation to take a 21 year lease with a sum equivalent to an 8 per cent dividend. With this came control of the Barnsley Canal which the C&HN had in turn leased since 1854. The A&CN also continued developing its own line and works. Cargo-carrying tugs came into operation during the 1850s. Pollington Lock, the first up from Goole Docks, was extended by three times its length so that trains of six boats behind a single tug could be used; the 206 ft long by 22 ft wide lock was reopened in October 1860. The locks further upstream – Whitley, Bulhome, Ferrybridge and Castleford – were all similarly treated to enable the passage of tugged trains all the way from Goole to Castleford. The programme of lock extensions was continued to Wakefield (by 1869) and Leeds (by 1873). At the same time, the navigation's engineer, W.H. Bartholomew, introduced compartment boats coupled together into trains towed by a steam tug. These vessels, known as 'Tom Puddings', were to become the workhorses of the A&CN with as many as thirty or forty 'tubs' included in a single train. Although not immediately successful, the use of Tom Puddings gradually restored the A&CN's coal traffic so that by 1897 the Goole Canal carried some 473,061 tons

A loaded train of Tom Puddings makes its way along the Aire & Calder Navigation, probably in the 1950s

National Coal Board

compared with 313,449 tons in 1845. There was also a notable increase in imported timber although the grain-carrying business declined – mostly due to the greater levels of imports from the Prairies into Liverpool.

The end of the century saw the A&CN still developing its line and its port at Goole. New docks were built and in 1884 the A&CN became the conservators of a stretch of the Lower Ouse. They were thus able to improve the stretch to the Trent thereby allowing larger ships to reach Goole. The cost of the work was enabled by the 1884 Act with the creation of £950,000 of debenture stock. By 1902 all the locks were built to a standard 215 ft by 22 ft by 9 ft deep. This enabled Tom Puddings to work the locks in trains of nineteen boats in one movement. The New Junction Canal, which had been suggested by the Stainforth & Keadby Canal Company in 1833, was opened in 1905. The canal, which was built as a joint venture with the Sheffield & South Yorkshire Navigation, runs for 5^1/$_2$ miles from the Goole Canal near Newbridge to Kirk Bramwith on the S&SYN. Although it cost £300,000 to build, trade along the line was slow to develop.

The late nineteenth and early twentieth centuries were otherwise a good period for the A&CN. From an allocation to dividends of just £40,500 in 1880, the figures rose to £60,000 in 1891 and £83,700 in 1909. By 1910 the Tom Pudding compartment boats were carrying 1,297,226 tons of coal p.a.; more than double the figure carried ten years earlier. This rose to 1,563,789 tons out of a total of 2,750,000 tons of coal in total. There were also increased shipments of timber and corn. In 1913 the line moved a total of 3,597,921 tons of cargo.

The First World War caused a slight hiccup in the fortunes of the A&CN; toll revenue of £119,415 in 1913 falling to £33,567 in 1919 before recovering to £71,146 by 1925. But even in the 1930s the committee had sufficient confidence in the future to undertake some further improvements to the Lower Ouse and to construct a new lock (Ocean Lock) from the line into the Ouse at Goole. The new lock could handle 4,000 ton ships. By the Second World War revenue had risen to £193,000 with more than 1³/₄ million tons of coal (increasingly being delivered to waterside power stations) and ³/₄ million tons of other cargo being moved annually.

The next significant phase of the A&CN's history started on 1 January 1948 when it was nationalized and put under the control of the British Transport Commission. The A&CN was probably the jewel in the new

Scene at the coal terminus at Newlands Basin, Stanley Ferry, probably in the early 1900s
The Boat Museum Archive

BTC's crown. Its future as a navigation was never a matter of debate and, unlike most waterways, trade along the line was actively developed. Shipments in 1953 topped 2¹/₂ million tons and in 1962 exceeded 3 million tons with revenue at £357,725. At that stage coal still remained the most important trade comprising nearly 71 per cent of the cargo moved. Such activity allowed British Waterways to continue upgrading the facilities along the line. In the late 1960s some minor amendments to the course and capacity of the navigation were made. The line to Leeds, now 10 ft deep, could take 500 ton boats measuring 180 ft by 18 ft 6 in. The line to Castleford was again upgraded to handle craft to 700 tons, and since 1978 the entire line to Leeds has been able to take boats of this size. All the locks on the main line have been electrified. Push tugs were introduced in 1967 and are used to deliver coal to the massive Ferrybridge power station. The tugs push compartment boats each 56 ft long by 17 ft 3 in wide which are able to carry 165 tons. They are pushed three at a time between colliery loading staithes and the power station where they are lifted out of the water and upturned to discharge the load (a process that takes less than nine minutes). Tonnage through the 1970s and '80s still exceeded 2 million tons although toll revenue in 1971 was down to £146,392. The Ferrybridge power station complex alone was receiving 1¹/₂ million tons of coal a year in the late 1970s. Even though the last Tom Puddings plied the line in March 1992 (from collieries at Kippax Lock near Mickletown to Ferrybridge B), Ferrybridge C still receives coal via the navigation. Cawood-Hargreaves moves coal using high-sided 'pan' barges that are towed by tugs.

The A&CN is one of the nation's most successful commercial waterways and it is still thriving to this day. Who knows, in an increasingly environmentally conscious world, the navigation may be well positioned as a viable alternative to road transport and all true sceptics can say 'I told you so'.

The Walk

Start and finish:	Knottingley railway station (OS ref: SE 491236)
Distance:	4¹/₄ miles/7 km
Map:	OS Landranger 105 (York)
Car park:	Knottingley railway station
Public transport:	Knottingley is on the Leeds to Goole line (enquiries: (0532) 457676)

From the railway station, walk out to the main road and turn right. Go straight on at the traffic lights and walk on past a row of shops and the Bay

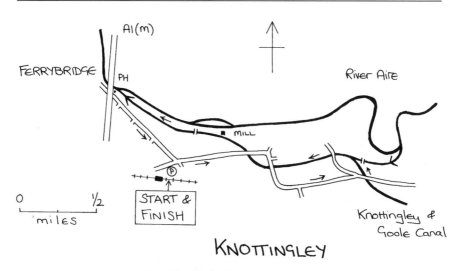

KNOTTINGLEY

The Aire & Calder Navigation

Horse pub. After passing the Working Men's Club, the road crosses the navigation for the first time. Continue around a right bend into Weeland Road. The road crosses the navigation for a second time and bends left to pass Rockware Glass works. At a road junction continue straight on along a road signposted to Goole. This passes the Lamb Inn and John Harker 'ship-builders and repairers'. After crossing the navigation for the third time, turn left along a small lane signposted to Willow Garth Nature Reserve.

The waterway to your left is the Aire & Calder Navigation or, if you prefer, the Knottingley and Goole Canal. This is the line which took the waterway to the then new port of Goole and thus bypassed the former route along the River Aire to Airmyn or along both the Aire and the Selby Canal to Selby. The new line opened in July 1826 with much celebration. A procession of four steam packets and fifty sailing vessels made their way from Ferrybridge to Goole. They were accompanied by bands playing music and crowds waving flags. Starting at 10 a.m., the cavalcade reached Goole at 4 p.m. to be welcomed by a twenty-one gun salute and, for the VIPs at least, a slap-up meal at the Banks Arms Hotel.

Towpathers who venture along the A&CN today will feast in a slightly different way and that is in the sight of working vessels. Nowhere else in any of the three *Canal Walks* books in this series (which cover forty-six different canals) will you be able to see a line being used for the purpose for which it was built. There are broadly two types of vessel and you are almost certain to meet one or other and most likely both. The first group are the tankers. One line is run by Whitfleet Limited (part of the Whitaker Group) and includes vessels which sail under the names of *Humber Energy* (which passed me as I made my way down the lane), *Humber Navigator, Humber Jubilee* and *Humber Progress*. These boats ship loads of petroleum products from the Humberside refineries to various storage depots along the A&CN. The tankers can move up to 650 tons per load. The second type of tanker is the effluent tanker such as the Dean & Dyball Shipping *Trentaire*. *Trentaire* is presently on contract to Yorkshire Water to ship effluent sludge (some 450 tons at a time) from Knostrop (near Leeds) to Goole where the contents are transhipped for subsequent dumping at sea. *Trentaire* has a sister ship, *Trentcal*. Both were built in Le Havre in 1957 and were originally designed to carry wine. This may be considered to be a bit of a come-down but, at just over 180 ft long by 18 ft wide, they are the largest vessels that regularly ply the A&CN.

The lane leads to a small bridge, Trundles Bridge, over a junction canal to the River Aire. Turn right here briefly to follow the line round to see Bank Dole Lock, the first on this, the old, route to Selby. This short link between the Knottingley & Goole Canal and the River Aire was built at the same time as the K&GC to allow traffic to pass on to Selby and thence to York. Just beyond the lock, the junction between the cut and the river can be seen. Return to the bridge and walk on (following a signpost for the 'Knottingley Canal Walk') along a grassy area with Harker's boatyard on the far bank. Harker's, established in 1929, once built and maintained barges and coasters here although when I passed, the site appeared quiet and declining. At one stage Harker's operated their own large fleet of bulk fuel tankers.

The towpath goes under Shepherd's Bridge and then on under Caslane Bridge. Just after this, on the opposite bank, is the Steam Packet pub followed by the site of Rockware Glass, manufacturers of a wide variety of bottles and jars. At one time the factory had its supplies of silica sand delivered by barge; some of this being specially shipped in from Belgium.

We continue under Jackson's Bridge before the canal swings right to go under Gagg's Bridge and on past Kings Mill. Today the mill hides behind high fences and trade is continued with the aid of numerous, noisy lorries. In former times the mill received its grain supplies from the navigation. And before that it used the River Aire, which is just beyond the mill buildings to the right, as a source of power for its water-wheels.

After going under another road bridge, Mill Bridge, we walk along an increasingly narrow stretch between the A&CN to the left and the River Aire to the right. The land around here has been treated to an environmental improvement scheme that is being run by the Wakefield Groundwork Trust. Despite the proximity of industry and the ever-present rumble from the nearby A1(M), it's a pleasant airy spot with the Ferrybridge power stations acting as a clear book-end on the horizon. A weir on the Aire brings the level of the river up to that of the canal and at one point we cross sluice-gates between the canal and the river. When

The 460 ft long
Ferrybridge Flood Lock at
Kellingley

offered the choice, take the left-hand path which will bring you round to
Ferrybridge Flood Lock. It is an enormous structure at 460 ft long. About
two-thirds of the way along is a lock-keeper's lookout box. Cross the canal
via the footbridge at the far end of the lock from where there are splendid
views back downstream along the length of the lock and upstream towards
the A1(M) flyover and the power stations. If you're lucky, you may well be
able to watch the second type of commonly seen commercial boats as they
manoeuvre through the lock: the coal boats that deliver fuel to the
Ferrybridge power stations.

There are nine Cawood-Hargreaves coal barge trains altogether and they
are numbered CH101–109. Each train can carry 500 tons of coal from the
Kellingley deep mine to the Ferrybridge C station in three containers. When
empty, the vessels float high on the water but when full they wallow along,
only barely above the surface. On arrival at Ferrybridge, each compartment
is lifted out of the water and poured into a large hopper from where the coal
is moved along a conveyor to the station. Ferrybridge C, I'm assured, can

A Cawood-Hargreaves coal barge train passes through Kellingley on its way to the Ferrybridge power stations that are in the distance

burn 1,000 tons of coal an hour. About 40 per cent of this is supplied by these boats which are the natural successors to William Bartholomew's Tom Puddings which went out of service as recently as March 1992.

On the far side of the footbridge, turn right to walk along the front to the Golden Lion pub. Here the River Aire and the Knottingley and Goole Canal form a junction. Before 1826 traffic took the Aire route to the River Ouse. To your left, as you look at the navigation, is a fine view as far as the eighteenth-century road bridge which is now limited to pedestrian traffic and probably grateful for it.

To return to the railway station, turn left and walk up the hill to the traffic lights. Turn right to reach the station.

Further Explorations

The A&CN is not a haven for walkers. A lot of the more easterly stretches pass through rather bland, flat landscape while much of the more interesting westerly end is sadly not accessible. Indeed, I was told by British Waterways that it was dangerous! Hopefully one day it will be possible to walk from Wakefield to Knottingley but at present this is not feasible.

Despite this, the stretch of canal at Stanley Ferry is worth a visit and a mooch. Stanley Ferry can be found on OS Landranger 104 (Leeds & Bradford) at ref: SE 355231. There is a car park at the Ferry Boat Inn. From there, steps lead up to the pub and to the towpath. Just across the waterway are a line of small terrace houses which were built by the A&CN company in the 1880s to house the banksmen and their families.

Originally the A&CN between Castleford and Wakefield used the River Calder and it was opened for traffic in 1701. There had been a crossing over the river since Roman times and a ferry operational since the seventeenth century at the latest. Stanley Ferry had thus grown into a small community which included a hostelry for passing traders. By the mid-1820s traffic along the A&CN was burgeoning and it was decided to upgrade this section of the waterway. Thomas Telford was engaged to improve the route and he did so by producing a characteristically straight course which reduced the distance between Castleford and Wakefield by 4 miles. As part of those improvements Telford took his new line over the meandering Calder at Stanley Ferry.

Before taking a closer look at the crossing, it is well worth having a stroll along Telford's oh-so-straight waterway. To do so, turn right and walk along the line to the footbridge, which in one book on my shelf is called Ramsden's Swing Bridge. Once across, turn right and walk on to pass two bridges to Broadreach Lock. The stretch of the canal here has been extensively reclaimed and was the site of the 1992 National Waterways Festival. It was formerly the site of various buildings and yards associated with Parkhills colliery. Navigation-side loading staithes were used to charge waiting barges with coal for shipment to Hull, Grimsby, Goole, and even London. The staithes were still operational in 1975 when coal was shipped out by the Leeds Co-op. The colliery closed in December 1982. Just beyond the lock, the canal and the River Calder rejoin en route for Wakefield which makes itself evident to the right.

Once at the end there's nothing for it but to return along the towpath. Don't cross the footbridge initially but continue past the cottages and on to see where the A&CN crosses the Calder. There are actually two aqueducts here. The original, built as part of Telford's scheme, was designed by George Leather. It has two bow-shaped, cast-iron arcs that support the trough on either side while the ends are supported on stone abutments. The rather fine structure carries a trough that is 165 ft long, 24 ft wide, 8 ft 6 in deep and which holds 940 tons of water. Work on the aqueduct started in November 1834 with iron cast by William Graham & Co. of Milton Ironworks, Elsecar, on foundations constructed by another contractor, Hugh MacIntosh. The aqueduct was opened on 9 August 1839 at a cost of nearly £50,000. It is now scheduled as an ancient monument.

By the start of the 1970s the old aqueduct was suffering, both as a result of subsidence and due to being repeatedly rammed by passing vessels. As part of the upgrading of the Wakefield section to a 700 ton standard, a new aqueduct was opened in November 1981. Although decidedly more utilitarian than its neighbour, the new structure has a deeper draught and allows larger vessels to make their way upstream. It was designed by Husband & Co. and is 237 ft long, 29^1/$_2$ ft wide and a little over 14 ft deep.

As you return back to the footbridge, you will note the basin on the pub side of the navigation. This is Stanley Ferry Basin (or the Lofthouse Basin). It was originally built in 1840 and was served by a narrow gauge railway which brought coal from Lofthouse down to the canal. The railway was closed in 1924 when lorries started to do the work, and traffic as a whole came to a stop in the 1940s. Since then the basin has been used for various purposes including an oil distribution depot and a wheat wharf.

Stanley Ferry is also the site of a British Waterways yard. This too has a history that dates back to the earliest days of the line. In 1833, when the Calder Cut was being built, the land purchase included the area between the waterway and the access road to the ferry. The land was leased for a while to a firm of boat builders who constructed a dry-dock and various buildings. In 1873 the operation was taken over by the A&CN as its principal repair yard and, with certain additions, it remains much the same today.

Recross the canal at the footbridge to visit the pub and to return to the car.

Further Information

While there is no A&CN society as such, the Inland Waterways Association has its West Riding branch based in Leeds. The address of the head office in London is given in Appendix B.

For historical information on both the navigation and the vessels that use it, the standard work is:

Smith, P.L., *The Aire & Calder Navigation*. Wakefield Historical Publications, 1987.

2
THE BRIDGEWATER CANAL
Worsley to Barton

Introduction

The Bridgewater Canal has the accolade of being the first in England to be built under the powers of a canal Act. Perhaps more importantly, it was THE model for those that came after. Once the success of the Bridgewater was evident then the rest were almost bound to follow. And it was a success. It was talk of the profits being earned on the Bridgewater that drove otherwise well-adjusted minds into canal mania.

The original line of the Bridgewater runs from Worsley in north-west Manchester through Eccles (where it crosses the Manchester Ship Canal on the Barton Aqueduct) via Trafford Park into the centre of the city at Castlefield. Later the canal was extended west from Worsley to Leigh where it now forms a junction with the Leeds & Liverpool Canal. At Trafford Park, a second, more southerly, line leaves a junction with the original to head through Sale to Altrincham and Lymm. It then passes through the outskirts of Warrington before meeting the Trent & Mersey Canal at Preston Brook. The route then turns abruptly west to its modern-day terminus in central Runcorn. In a more glorious age, two lines of locks ran down the hill to the docks and the River Mersey.

The town canals aren't the natural habitat for the dedicated walker but yard for yard they are usually the more interesting ones. The Bridgewater is no exception. Besides, going to Worsley is almost a pilgrimage.

History

In 1736, with the Mersey & Irwell Navigation nearly complete, the M&IN company started to consider the possibility of building a waterway to the coalfields around Wigan. The original plan had been that the Douglas Navigation would serve the area but the construction work had been slow and the M&IN saw coal deliveries to Manchester as a potentially important trade. The M&IN engineer, Thomas Steers, was asked to carry out a survey of Worsley Brook with a view to making it navigable to Worsley with a new cut to Booth's Bank (towards Wigan). An Act was passed in 1737 but with construction of the Douglas Navigation once again under way, the project went no further.

By the time the third Duke of Bridgewater succeeded to the title in 1748, exploitation of the Wigan coalfield was increasing and many new turnpike roads were being built. The idea of a canal from the coalfield into Manchester was raised by a group of businessmen from the city in 1753. A line was proposed to run from Wigan via Leigh and Worsley to Eccles and Salford. William Taylor undertook a survey and a bill was put to Parliament. Although lost, the idea stayed with the young duke's agent, John Gilbert, and his guardian, Earl Gower. Both had industrial interests in Worsley and the earl had already employed James Brindley to survey a line that would become the Trent & Mersey Canal. The duke must have been impressed by the idea of a canal. In 1758 he visited his Worsley estates in order to assess the feasibility of a waterway to carry his coal directly into central Manchester, and in 1759 he purchased a tract of land in Salford with the view of making it the southern terminus of the planned canal.

The duke's scheme was for a level canal from Worsley to Salford with, if possible, a connection with the Irwell. When preparing the bill, it is widely recognized that the duke had learnt from the failure of the 1753–4 Bill and addressed many of the issues that were raised in opposition at that time. He promised that canal-delivered coal would be cheaper than that brought by road and promised to detail the price (not more than 4d. a hundredweight) before the bill was submitted. Lime and manure were to be carried free. The water supply would come entirely from Worsley Brook (there had previously been objections to extraction from the Irwell). The cost of the entire enterprise would be met from his own pocket. Interestingly, the duke's bill not only included details of a line from Salford to Worsley but also a second canal from Worsley to Hollins Ferry on the M&IN.

The Act, with no opposition, was passed on 23 March 1759 and the construction work began almost immediately. James Brindley was appointed engineer with John Gilbert overseeing the operation on behalf of the duke. By the beginning of 1760, there were already two miles of waterway from Worsley to Patricroft and two miles of the line towards Hollins Ferry which reached to Botany Bay Wood just north of Irlam.

Work had also begun within the colliery at Worsley where an underground canal system was to take the specially constructed boats, later to be known as 'starvationers', virtually to the coal face. The boats were typically

Starvationers at Delph Mine, Worsley, *c.* 1910

Ware/The Boat Museum Archive

47 ft long by 4¹/₂ ft wide and had prominent 'ribs'. When the system was fully operational, a train of five boats was pulled by a horse or a pair of mules into Manchester. The underground tunnels were 10 ft wide with a headroom of about 8 ft. The tunnels were built with loading bays and passing spaces and there were two other canals at different depths. These didn't connect directly with the main line but were able to convey coal to it via vertical shafts through which coal was delivered to waiting starvationers. The boats were propelled from the mine by opening a sluice and washing them out. A third underground canal, from Walkden, was connected to the main line via a 151 yd long underground inclined plane. Eventually there were to be more than 30 miles of underground tunnel at Worsley.

By this time, there had been a modification to the original line into Manchester. The new route was to pass from Patricroft over the Irwell via an aqueduct, over Trafford Moss and then on to a terminus which was eventually settled at Castlefield. The Hollins Ferry branch was dropped and never completed. This change of plan was enabled by an Act in March 1760. The aqueduct over the Irwell was opened on 17 July 1761 and boats, much to the apparent disbelief of the onlookers, sailed over the river with 'not a single drop of water' oozing through the masonry to the river below. By December 1761, the line had reached Stretford and, on 1 August 1765, the first wharf at Castlefield was operational.

While the main line was being completed, the duke was hatching his scheme for an extension of the Bridgewater Canal that would compete directly with the M&IN to Liverpool. Brindley had already surveyed the route by January 1762 when the duke published a pamphlet on the scheme in which he described the M&IN as 'imperfect, expensive and precarious'. The duke's line, 9 miles shorter than the M&IN route passed west from Longford Bridge, over the River Mersey and Sale Moor to Altrincham. The line then crossed the River Bollin to Lymm. The last stretch continued westwards, descending by a flight of ten locks to the Mersey at Hempstones, a point on the Mersey to the east of Runcorn. The new line was to be supplied from the same Worsley springs that kept the main line in water. The scheme was opposed vigorously, and unsuccessfully, by the M&IN. The western end of the line was altered by an Act of 1766 so that it joined the Trent & Mersey Canal at Preston Brook before making its way to the Mersey. With this, the locks were moved to Runcorn.

On 21 March 1776 the line to Runcorn was open for traffic and the duke had a canal that connected Manchester with the Midlands via the T&M as well as a route to the profitable coal market of Liverpool. Hadfield & Biddle estimate the cost of the canal to this point at approximately £80,000. The duke, who by this time had been forced to borrow to complete his scheme, was soon more than well repaid. His income on freight carriage between Liverpool and Manchester alone in the period from 1770 to 1779 was £21,472. The two years 1780 and 1781 earnt him £7,381. And these figures do not include the sale of the duke's own coal in central Manchester; a trade that grew dramatically.

To support the trade in Liverpool, the duke purchased land on the banks of the Mersey and had his own dock and warehouses built. There was also a healthy passenger traffic between Warrington and Manchester. For a fare of 10d. basic or 2s. 6d. first class, patrons could spend five hours being liberally supplied with tea and cakes while journeying between the two towns. The service was a popular one with annual receipts in the late 1780s approaching £3,000. By this time, the canal was carrying about 265,000 tons of freight p.a. of which 64,000 tons was coal; over 30 per cent of the traffic was from Liverpool. Annual receipts for this period averaged over £60,000.

By the turn of the nineteenth century, the English canal network was beginning to take shape. In 1804 the Bridgewater had a junction with the Rochdale Canal at Castlefield; a link which opened the way for Worsley coal to reach markets to the east as well as providing a route for limestone and merchandise coming west. Castlefield was now frequented by no fewer than twelve different carrying companies including the duke's own, Pickfords and Hugh Henshall & Co. (which was owned by the T&M). By 1821 there were twenty-one companies and it was possible to catch a fly-boat all the way to London. An additional line north was forged when the Leigh branch of the Leeds & Liverpool Canal joined the Bridgewater at Leigh. This link had started life when the duke obtained an Act in 1795 enabling the extension of the line from Worsley to Leigh. The route opened in 1799 and was joined with the L&L in 1820 when that company built a branch south. The trade from Manchester to Runcorn, however, was one that was bitterly fought for by the M&IN who, by 1804, had a new cut all the way into Runcorn. To work this, the M&IN introduced a steam packet which could whisk passengers from Manchester to Runcorn in just eight hours (the Bridgewater boat took nine) for immediate transfer to the Liverpool boat. This competition seems to have halted the otherwise ever increasing growth in receipts along the duke's canal. The duke responded by ending an agreement on rates and by raising tolls sharply. There was then a sudden and dramatic rise in profits from an average of £24,441 p.a. for 1797–9 to £50,736 p.a. for 1803–5.

The great canal duke died on 8 March 1803 and his canal property passed to the Marquess of Stafford. The duke willed that a group of trustees be established to further the interests of the collieries and the canal line which were to be managed by Robert Bradshaw. The change had little affect on the business during a period of relative calm. For the years 1806–24, receipts and profit levels remained static at approximately £120,000 and £45,000 respectively. The Bridgewater and the M&IN had a toll agreement for the prosperous Manchester–Liverpool route and it was accepted that if one company altered their rates then the other would follow suit. The two companies also followed each other in terms of new facilities. After the M&IN had built itself a substantial new basin at Runcorn, the Bridgewater built a second line of locks at its terminus in the town. The tidal lock was then extended and a new slate wharf added.

The first suggestion of a railway between Liverpool and Manchester was seen in a newspaper on 2 October 1822. The Bridgewater and the M&IN were united in their opposition to the scheme which both recognized as potentially damaging to their interests. The opposition was successful and the Liverpool & Manchester Railway Bill of 1825 was defeated. The Marquess of Stafford, however, was already coming down in favour of the idea of railed ways as the answer to the transport problems of the nineteenth century. He decided to support the new railway and to invest £100,000 (20 per cent of the capital) in it. As if to salve his own conscience, he also invested £40,000 in improving facilities along the Bridgewater. The M&IN was obviously displeased at this change of heart and said so but by then the battle was lost. The Act that enabled the historic Liverpool & Manchester

Railway to be built was passed on 1 May 1826. It was opened on 15 September 1830.

The waterway companies responded to the new competition by reducing their tolls, albeit without panic. Bradshaw must have found himself in a difficult position and was unable to form an alliance with the M&IN to control rates. It appears, however, that he remained a firm supporter of canal transport despite the sentiments of his employer. Bradshaw reduced tolls in order to maintain trade, but with a consequent slight reduction in receipts (from £175,997 in 1830 to £142,251 in 1833) and a substantial fall of profits (from £47,650 to £17,473).

When Lord Stafford died in 1833, ownership of the collieries and the canal passed to Lord Francis Egerton, the Marquess' second son, and James Sothern became manager. The two new incumbents were to often differ over policy. Egerton was keen to produce agreements with the railway and the M&IN over toll rates; Sothern wasn't. It wasn't until 1837 that Egerton was able to buy Sothern out and replace him with James Loch (as superintendent). The three companies then stopped a damaging series of rate-cut rounds and a kind of harmony was installed. In 1838 a junction was formed between the canal and the M&IN at Castlefield (via the Hulme Locks). This was presumably à boon to both lines but the construction of the Manchester & Salford Junction Canal (across central Manchester) to link the M&IN with the Rochdale, bypassed the Bridgewater junction at Castlefield and must thus have been a blow to Bridgewater prospects. In the event the M&SJC (which was bought by the M&IN) was not a great success and had little effect on the Bridgewater.

The agreement lasted until 1840 when the M&IN saw brighter prospects outside the alliance than in. It had forged a link with the Manchester & Leeds Railway, had plans for turning its line into a ship canal, and felt that it had a strong competitive base. The other two partners retaliated and the M&IN was forced to rejoin the pact. However, by December 1841, it was the Liverpool & Manchester Railway who saw its share of the business falling and who unilaterally reduced its cotton rates. This was followed in 1842 by an agreement between the LMR and the Manchester & Leeds for through rail traffic in direct competition with the waterways. By this time the average annual tonnages for each company's trade between Manchester and Liverpool were: Bridgewater 200,856; M&IN 141,813; and LMR 164,625. Although another rates agreement was made in 1843, vigorous unseemly competition between the three companies soon returned. The only solution, as James Loch realized, was for the Bridgewater to buy the M&IN and they duly did so on 17 January 1846 following an Act of 1845. The price was £400,000 although Egerton (or Lord Ellesmere as he had become) also took on a debt of £110,000. Funds were raised in bonds and by borrowing on mortgage but the Bridgewater was still doing well enough to afford the purchase. Profit in 1844 amounted to more than £85,000 with nearly 1,300,000 tons of cargo being carried along the line. About a quarter of this trade was carried by the Bridgewater's own carrying fleet.

Despite this success, James Loch was already reviewing the possibility of selling both the trustees' waterways to a consortia interested in converting them into railways, ship canals or both. Railway competition had been ever more serious during the late 1840s and by January 1850, a new agreement with the London & North Western Railway (into which the LMR had been absorbed in 1846) forced the trustees to accept 50 per cent of the Liverpool–Manchester traffic as against 66:33 in previous agreements. The canals going over the Pennines were by now all railway owned; a fact which further weighed against the Bridgewater trustees.

The one area of the canal's trade that was burgeoning was its carrying business which was now operating into the Midlands. It was thus opportune for James Loch to start discussions with the Great Western Railway who was looking to establish a carrying link into the north-west. But agreement on a lease or sale of the line to the GWR was not forthcoming, and when Loch died in 1855 no agreement was impending.

With Loch's death, Lord Ellesmere's third son, the Hon. Algernon Egerton became superintendent. This change of management brought about a change in attitude towards the railways. The canal would no longer be looking for railway associations or take-overs but would seek to strengthen its links with other waterways and build a viable long-distance trade. The 1¹/₄ mile long Runcorn & Weston Canal, which ran from the town to a basin at Weston Point a little further along the coast towards the Weaver Navigation, was opened in 1859. Improvements were made at Runcorn Docks with a new large tidal basin completed in 1860. Similar improvements were made to the trustees' docks at Liverpool.

In 1870 the Bridgewater carried 2,490,715 tons of cargo with about 44 per cent being handled by the trustees' carrying companies or associated companies. Despite this evident high level of trade, the trustees continued to seek a railway association. In 1871 the chairmen of two railway companies, Sir Edward Watkin and W.P. Price of the Manchester, Sheffield & Lincolnshire Railway and the Midland Railway respectively, formed a new company, the Bridgewater Navigation Company, and purchased all of the canal interests of the trustees for £1,115,000. The deal was completed on 3 July 1872 with Edward Leader Williams appointed as general manager.

The new canal company set about bringing its possession into the steam age. Leader Williams introduced steam tugs, which could each tow three barges on the lockless section of the line from Runcorn. Perhaps more significantly, the company looked to improving the now declining M&IN. Accommodation at Runcorn was improved including the opening of the Fenton Dock in July 1875. By this time the Runcorn complex was handling

500,000 tons of cargo p.a. including exports of salt, coal, pitch and earthenware, and imports of flint, china clay, iron, grain and sand. The dock complex covered 16 acres of water and 37 acres of quay.

Business along the BNC's waterways in 1884 was still brisk. Some 2,815,018 tons of cargo were moved along the lines about half of which was shipped into the estuary, and 800,000 tons of cargo, mostly coal, crossed the Barton Aqueduct towards Manchester with little or no business taking the return route. By now just 30 per cent of the traffic was carried by carriers associated with the BNC. Traffic in and out of Runcorn was still totalling about 500,000 tons p.a. The BNC was able to pay 8 per cent dividend throughout the 1880s with profits hovering around £60,000 p.a.

Despite the profits, a key threat to the BNC arose during the course of the 1880s. The Act for the Manchester Ship Canal was passed on 6 August 1885. The Act not only enabled the construction of the new waterway but provided powers for the new company to purchase its potential rival, the BNC, for £1,710,000. The purpose behind the move was that the MSC was to be built mostly along the course of the old M&IN. The ship canal was open to traffic on 1 January 1894 and officially declared open by Queen Victoria in the following May. As part of the new MSC, Brindley's old

Brindley's original Barton Aqueduct which was demolished to make way for the present swinging aqueduct in 1894

Ware/The Boat Museum Archive

Bridgewater Canal Barton Aqueduct was demolished and replaced by the present swing aqueduct which was designed by Leader Williams.

Although the MSC developed a significant level of new business of its own, it was inevitable that there would be a drop in traffic along the Manchester to Runcorn line of the Bridgewater. However, this was more than adequately compensated by the business created for the Bridgewater at the Manchester terminus where the old canal formed a valuable link with the Rochdale and the line to the Leigh branch and Wigan. The continued high levels of carriage along the route to the Leeds & Liverpool meant that, by the time of the First World War, carriage was still nearly 2,000,000 tons p.a. But thereafter, the business declined. By the time of the Second World War, tonnage was down to just 815,391. In the 1960s, by which time the canal no longer reached down its western locks to the Runcorn Docks, traffic was down to a quarter of a million tons. Trafford Park power station continued to receive its coal deliveries by barge until 1972 and by 1974 all the freight traffic had gone. The Bridgewater Canal was not nationalized in 1948 and is still owned by the Manchester Ship Canal Company. Today it is a popular holiday route and part of the well-known Cheshire Ring.

The Walk

Start and finish:	Worsley Green (OS ref: SD 747004)
Distance:	5^1/$_2$ miles/9 km
Map:	OS Landranger 109 (Manchester)
Car park:	Near A572 roundabout
Public transport:	British Rail Patricroft

From the A572 roundabout (near junction 13 of the M62), take the B5211 road to Eccles and park in the free car park which is about 100 yd after the turning. Leave the car park and turn right to go over the canal bridge, Worsley Bridge, in Barton Road. Before going down to the canal, cross the road to admire the view. Here is the Bridgewater, glowing yellow-orange with the iron hydroxide (ochre) that has leached from the old coal mines.

Before starting the main walk, pass down the left-hand side of the canal to walk in front of the Packet House with the canal to the right. From here in the summer months, visitors can take canal boat trips. In fact, this has been the embarkation point for travellers along the canal since the Duke of Bridgewater's time. Packet-boats operated to destinations as far as Runcorn, Warrington and Manchester. In 1841 a packet-boat left Worsley for central Manchester at ten in the morning and six in the evening. The trip took just

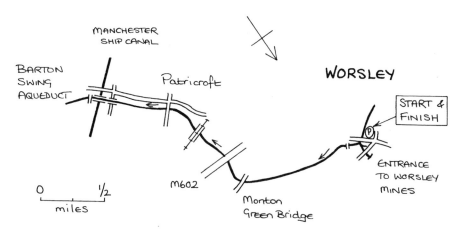

MANCHESTER SHIP CANAL

BARTON SWING AQUEDUCT

Patricroft

WORSLEY

START & FINISH

ENTRANCE TO WORSLEY MINES

M602

Monton Green Bridge

0 ½ miles

The Bridgewater Canal

two hours and cost 9d. first class or 6d. second. The fine, and much photographed, Packet House, by the way, was built in the late eighteenth century. The Tudoresque frontage is strictly Victorian imitation, being added in the 1850s under the guidance of the Earl of Ellesmere.

Continue on and across the small footbridge (called the ABC Bridge because it has twenty-six planks) to an island with the oldest building in the district, built in 1725 – and hence before the canal. In the 1760s the build-ing housed a nailmaker's workshop and from that it takes its name to this day. Worsley Road Bridge is to the right. Underneath the bridge are entrances to some underground rooms reputed to be stables for the horses used in the mine's horse-gins. Walk on with the Nailmaker's Workshop to the right up to the road. Cross here and bear left to School Brow. Here on the left is The Delph and the entrance to the Duke of Bridgewater's mines. The Delph itself was once a sandstone quarry and much of the stone was used to build many of the canal's bridges.

There are two entrances to the 30 miles of tunnels that form the Worsley coalfields. The tunnels were probably started when the canal was first built and were still being extended into the 1840s. In their heyday, the underground canals became quite a tourist attraction and many good and famous folk came to take a subterranean trip. As mentioned earlier, the underground canals were on three levels, connected partly by an inclined plane. The tunnels are mostly brick-lined and still in relatively good condition. The starvationer boats used in the tunnels were moved primarily by opening a sluice which then washed them out, although some legging or simple pushing must have been needed in places. Once outside, the full boats were towed into Manchester by horses and empty ones legged into the tunnels along the now-still waters. The starvationers

A canal arm to The Delph off the Bridgewater Canal at Worsley

were last used in 1889 by which time a steam railway had been built. The Worsley field was last mined in the 1960s.

To start the main section of the walk, return to Worsley Road Bridge and cross the road. Take the steps to the left of the bridge near Bank Cottage. These lead down to the canal. Turn right to go under the bridge with the canal to your left. Here on the left is the canal entrance to The Delph as well as the Packet House.

The towpath leads round right and on with a fine-looking boat house on the opposite bank. This was built by Lord Ellesmere, the Duke of Bridgewater's great nephew, to house a royal barge built for Queen Victoria's visit in 1851. An information notice back at the Packet House tells the story of how the rain-soaked crowds who attended the occasion were so noisy that they scared one of the horses pulling the royal barge, causing it to leap into the canal. History does not recall whether the queen was amused.

Go under the footbridge (which goes to the Worsley Green) with the Bridgewater Hotel to the right. The footbridge was built at the behest of the

Earl of Ellesmere in 1901. Just opposite Brinks Boats is an information notice that explains the history of the area. On the left are some dry-docks and on the right a converted granary. The granary was originally a forge with a water-wheel worked by Worsley Brook. The dry-docks date from the early 1760s and are reputed to be the earliest on the entire inland waterway system. Most of the barges that worked on the canal and in the mines were built here. Just beyond the granary on the right are the barely recognizable remains of some old limekilns.

The path goes through a gate and turns right along a very straight long embankment. The new houses on the left bank are on a site formerly occupied by colliery basins. The canal goes under Monton Green (road) Bridge, changes colour to the more normal canal green, and bends right to go past The Bargee Inn and Restaurant. On the right is a new residential development called 'The Waterside' (built on the site of an old textile mill building), and on the left a housing estate. The canal then goes under the M602. After this, on the right, is a still extant mill – Eccles Spinning and Manufacturing Co. Ltd – now used by the mail-order group Great Universal. The canal goes under a railway bridge (which carries the old Liverpool & Manchester Railway), past the Wellington pub and beyond, with the Barton Road close to the right. After Boat Building Services, continue under Patricroft Bridge with Bridgewater Mill looming from the left bank of the canal. Here is the diminuitive Packethouse Pub. The route continues with a basin to the left now occupied by the Worsley Cruising Club. One of the basin warehouses has an overhanging loading shelter. Shortly the towpath ends and walkers are forced onto the pavement. Continue on to traffic lights and then straight over the crossroads to reach the metal girder bridge which crosses the Manchester Ship Canal. Here on the left is the Barton Swing Aqueduct.

The Manchester Ship Canal was built on a scale larger than anything else attempted in England. It was opened on 1 January 1894 after seven years of construction and an expenditure of over £14 million. To make way for the new waterway, five railways were diverted and a whole series of new bridges were built to accommodate the required headroom of 70 ft. The canal was built to a depth of 26 ft (later deepened to 28 ft) and is capable of taking vessels of 10,000 tons. There are five sets of locks: at Mode Wheel (Salford), Barton, Irlam, Latchford and a sea lock at Eastham. Each set contains a large lock which measures 600 ft long by 65 ft wide together with a smaller version for tugs and other small vessels. The line was a phenomenal success, carrying millions of tons of cargo p.a. and turning Manchester into a major industrial city.

The swing aqueduct that takes the Bridgewater over the MSC is widely regarded as one of the wonders of Victorian engineering. Originally, Brindley had built a three-arched stone aqueduct here at Barton. Altogether (including the approaches) it was 600 ft long. The central arch spanned

57 ft and the two side arches were 32 ft each. It was 36 ft wide: 18 ft of waterway, 6 ft of puddled lining and the remainder packed with earth. With the advent of the MSC, the old aqueduct had to go and this new structure, designed by Edward Leader Williams, replaced it in 1894. The new aqueduct comprises a 235 ft long wrought-iron tank, 18 ft wide and 7 ft deep. To allow shipping to pass along the MSC, the aqueduct swings on a central pivot by means of sixty-four cast-iron rollers. This manoeuvre is undertaken with a full caisson of water and there are hydraulically operated lock-like gates at each end to seal the tank. The small gap between it and the canal side is bridged by a rubber-shod iron wedge which is moved into place by hydraulic dams. All this is worked from the control tower on the central pier. A close-up view of the aqueduct can be obtained by continuing over the bridge and turning left up a driveway and then left onto a path which leads to some steps and a viewing bridge.

The control tower of the Barton Swing Aqueduct that carries the Bridgewater over the Manchester Ship Canal near Eccles

It is possible to continue along the Bridgewater to Trafford Park and central Manchester; however, to return to Worsley, you can either catch one of the many buses that cross the MSC here or return by foot along the canal.

Further Explorations

There's a pleasant afternoon stroll of about 7 miles along the Bridgewater from Altrincham to the canal village of Lymm on the Greater Manchester/Cheshire borderlands (OS Landranger 109, ref: SJ 682873). I chose to park in the well-signposted free car park near the library in Lymm and then took the North Western bus no. 37 (enquiries: (061) 228 7811) to the bus station in Altrincham. From there, continue along New Road into Barrington Road. At a T-junction, turn right along Manchester Road to cross the canal just after Navigation Road. After passing over the canal (on Broadheath Bridge), walk into the car park of Halford's superstore and bear right around the Altrincham, Sale & District Sea Cadets' building to reach the canal. Turn right so that the canal is on the left.

The line from Manchester to Runcorn was the second phase of the construction of the Bridgewater Canal and was enabled by an Act of 1762. The canal was open to Altrincham and the first tolls were taken on 6 June 1766. Within the year, coal prices in Altrincham had halved. The line between here and the end of the walk, at Lymm, took three years to build and it wasn't until 1776 that the route to Runcorn was fully operational.

The towpath immediately passes under the Manchester Road and continues on with some industrial buildings to the left (including an old cotton warehouse with a covered loading bay) and some new DIY stores to right. Although for some distance the path is accompanied by industry and a new housing estate, after going under Seamon's Moss Bridge (at Oldfield Brow), the canal reaches countryside. After meandering around some open farmland, the line reaches Dunham Town at Dunham School Bridge (turn left here for the Axe and Cleaver pub) and then Dunham Town Bridge.

The canal now crosses the Bollin embankment; a high and surprisingly 'modern' feature for this, one of our oldest canals. It offers towpathers a fine airy position and good views over the surrounding countryside. En route we pass over three small aqueducts: Dunham Underbridge, the River Bollin and Bollington Underbridge. The embankment has not been without its problems. In 1971 the southern side near the Bollin Aqueduct collapsed. Although there was some debate as to whether the line would ever reopen, the company eventually built a 300 yd long concrete channel which was rewatered in 1973. The embankment also offers views left to the National Trust's Dunham Massey Hall.

At the end, the canal bends right to Agden Bridge. A straight section now leads past a series of mooring spaces and Lymm and Hesford Marinas. After crossing the B5159 via Burford Lane Underbridge (aqueduct), we pass Grantham's Bridge and then Lloyd Bridge on the outskirts of Oughtrington. It is now just a short distance to the A6144 bridge in Lymm which you'll recognize as it has a separate footbridge ably protected by lime-green railings.

The history of Lymm is closely linked with that of the canal. In the early nineteenth century, the town was an important stopping place for the Manchester to Runcorn (and hence Liverpool) packet-boat. The vessel stopped here for 15 minutes to allow passengers to stretch their legs and gain refreshment from a local hostelry before proceeding onwards. Reports suggest that more often than not all 120 seats were full for the journey which, in 1784, took $3^1/_2$ hours from Castlefield or $6^1/_2$ from Runcorn.

If you cross the bridge and continue along the right-hand bank, you will return to the library car park. In doing so, you pass over an aqueduct over Bradley Brook. Otherwise go left across the bridge into the village centre.

If you wish to visit the Manchester terminus of the canal at Castlefield Junction, see Further Explorations in the Rochdale Canal chapter.

Further Information

The canal was not privatized and hence is not managed by British Waterways. The owners are:

The Manchester Ship Canal Company,
Admin Building,
Queen Elizabeth II Dock,
Eastham,
Wirral L62 0BB.

There is no canal society as such but the Inland Waterways Association has a Manchester branch. For the address of the branch secretary contact IWA head office in London (see Appendix B).

For more details of the history of the Bridgewater:

Hadfield, C. and Biddle, G., *The Canals of North West England,* Vols. I and II. David & Charles, 1970.

3
THE CHESTERFIELD CANAL
Norwood Tunnel to Worksop

Introduction

The Chesterfield is, perhaps surprisingly, one of the earliest of the nation's canals. Surveyed originally by James Brindley, it is of similar vintage to the Oxford Canal. If you look closely, its age shows. You certainly wouldn't have caught Thomas Telford building the Shropshire Union along such a meandering line, and would he have shied clear of the straight course from Retford to Gainsborough? Of course, we can only guess at the answer and while we do, we can enjoy a magnificent waterway.

The Chesterfield Canal starts its life at West Stockwith where it forms a junction with the River Trent a few miles downstream from Gainsborough. From there the line heads south-west to pass to the west of Gringley on the Hill before turning south-east to Clayworth. After running south to the town of Retford, the canal heads west to Worksop where the current head of navigation is reached just short of Morse Lock. The now partially, or sometimes wholly, derelict line runs up to the summit pound and through the Norwood Tunnel. From the western portal of the tunnel, the line formerly descended through Killamarsh before heading south to Staveley and then west to its terminus at Chesterfield.

Here is a fine country walk along a canal on the verge of restoration. For that reason, it's worth walking now so that you can bore the grandchildren later with tales of what things used to be like in the bad old days.

History

For generations, the trade of Chesterfield together with the lead and stone of the eastern Derbyshire hills had been carried by road to Bawtry where it was loaded on to a boat, shipped down the River Idle to West Stockwith and then on to the River Trent for export to the rest of the country and, via Hull, the world. It was a cumbersome route and, at times, the River Idle was unnavigable through drought or flood.

With the opening of the Bridgewater Canal in 1763, the first flush of canal-building swept the country, and the businessmen of Chesterfield were soon discussing the potential for a canal to form a direct link between the town and the Trent. James Brindley, the canal engineer of the age, was approached in late 1768 and asked to undertake a survey. Brindley, who was building both the Trent & Mersey and the Staffordshire & Worcestershire at the time, delegated the initial inspection to one of his assistants, John Varley. The promoters of the new line initially asked Varley to survey a line from Chesterfield to Bawtry (which Brindley promptly costed at £100,000) but, with the growing interest of the people of Retford, a second route was surveyed by Varley in June 1769. The new line would run from Chesterfield to Worksop and Retford and then on to West Stockwith and the Trent; thus bypassing the River Idle altogether.

On 24 August 1769 the first public meeting was held at The Red Lion (now the Golden Ball) at Worksop. Brindley reported that a canal along the new line was practicable and estimated the cost as £95,000 or £105,000 if the eastern terminus were taken further up the Trent to Gainsborough. The meeting agreed on this latter option. However, by the following January, Brindley had decided that the West Stockwith Junction was to be preferred for reasons of cost, a faster completion date, the need for fewer locks and the avoidance of a tunnel through Castle Hill (between Retford and Gainsborough). The promoters of the new line suggested that it would be an important carrier of a range of different cargoes: coal, earthenware, lead, timber, millstones, limestone, roof tiles and gravel for mending roads. Of these, coal was always considered to be the most important. Brindley thought that with the opening of the canal, Derbyshire coal would be cheaper than the Yorkshire coal coming via the Don Navigation to Gainsborough. The canal would also import goods not regularly available in the land-locked towns of Chesterfield, Worksop and Retford: fine wool, rice, oils, wines, sugar, tobacco and fresh groceries.

Despite the opposition of John Lister, the owner of the navigation rights on the River Idle, a bill was presented on 23 January 1771 and the Act gained Royal Assent on 29 March. Powers were given to raise £100,000 in £100 shares with a further £50,000 should it be needed. Tolls, on what was to be a narrow boat canal, were set at 1¹/₂d. per ton on coal, lead, timber and stone and 1d. on lime. The project was promoted in London as well as locally and the issue was fully subscribed by July 1771. Brindley was appointed chief engineer at £300 p.a. but, as he was rather too over stretched to be regularly on-site, John Varley was made resident engineer with an annual salary of £100.

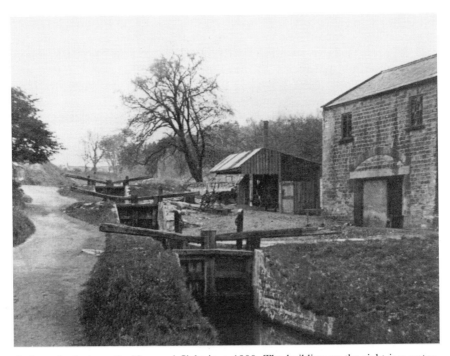

A three-rise lock on the Norwood flight in *c.* 1900. The building on the right is a water-powered sawmill

Dudley PL

The construction work started in the early autumn of 1771 with 300 men working on the two ends of the biggest engineering project along the line: the 2,850 yd long Norwood Tunnel. Work was also underway on the reservoir dam further up the hill at Pebley. Most of the construction work was undertaken by contractors who were employed for specific sections of digging or the building of particular bridges or locks. Brindley's plan was to complete the line section by section so that the canal company could open its waters for trade. This had the benefit of earning revenue as well as enabling the movement of some of the heavy construction materials that his contractors needed. Brindley's plans for the summer of 1772 included the amassing of the materials (primarily timber and stone) that were needed to build the flights of locks at each end of the summit pound: the Norwood flight westwards to Chesterfield and the Rother valley, and the Thorpe and Turnerwood Locks eastwards to Retford and the Ryton valley.

Sadly, in September 1772, James Brindley died while surveying the Caldon Canal. Initially John Varley was allowed to continue as acting chief engineer but Hugh Henshall, Brindley's brother-in-law, was appointed to the position at £250 p.a. With a less esteemed, if not necessarily less able, engineer, the company felt in a stronger bargaining position and insisted that its new appointee spend at least fifty-six days a year on site. It is perhaps a good job that it did. In the summer of 1773 Henshall found that some of the work at the Norwood Tunnel, a section contracted to John Varley's father and two brothers, wasn't up to standard. More examples of malpractice and lax management became apparent, further reflecting badly on the Varley family. It appears that John Varley was not directly blamed and the new regime under Henshall was able to make good the faults, rationalize the management and accounting systems and make excellent progress throughout 1774.

The earlier proposal that the Chesterfield should be a wide canal had been defeated, but now Retford Corporation and various shareholders from the town agreed to bear the expense of widening the line from Stockwith to Retford so that it could take the wide beam boats that worked the River Trent. This move was agreed by the canal company in May 1775 and the work got under way. Meanwhile, during the same month, Norwood Tunnel was officially opened. Three vessels sailed through the hill carrying about 300 people and a band who played appropriate airs. The journey took just over an hour from end to end. The new tunnel was 2,850 yd long, 9 ft 3 in wide and 12 ft high. It's said that the tunnel was so straight that it was possible to see the light at the other end. In that same month of May, work was proceeding to Chesterfield as well as on the Retford section of the line. By the beginning of April 1776 the canal was open from Killamarsh to the new basin at Stockwith. By August 1776 the canal was complete from the turnpike road at Norbriggs to Stockwith.

Following some difficulties in buying the necessary land at Stockwith, the lock into the Trent from the Chesterfield Canal was finally officially opened on 4 July 1777. In all, the line was 46 miles long with sixty-five locks. The day was celebrated with the arrival in Chesterfield of a boat from West Stockwith which, having been duly welcomed by a group of shareholders, was unloaded on to wagons. The shareholders, together with a band playing celebratory tunes, then led a procession into town. However, such festivities were short-lived. As early as September 1777 there were problems with Norwood Tunnel. Various individuals had dug coal from the ground over the tunnel and had damaged the roof by lessening the weight that compressed the arch. Mining subsidence was also to be a continuing problem over the years and was eventually to lead to the closure of the tunnel.

With the completion of the line, John Varley left the company and Richard Dixon, formerly the company's bookkeeper, took responsibility for engineering. Probably the first thing he had to consider was the construction of the Lady Lee arm for which permission had been given in March 1778. The arm was built for a Mr Gainsforth to link his stone quarry near

Worksop with the main line. Dixon also had to sort out the inadequate water supply on the Norwood Tunnel summit pound. In July 1779 penalties were imposed on empty or lightly laden boats travelling under 12 miles when using the locks. This unsatisfactory regulation was rescinded when Woodhall and Killamarsh Reservoirs were finished around 1790. Further capacity was added at Harthill by 1806.

The canal company also found its financial reservoirs equally inadequate. An attempt to raise additional funds by calls on shares was unsuccessful and £53,000 was borrowed on mortgage in order to complete the canal. The consequence of this was that a high proportion of the early trading profits were needed simply to service the loan. Furthermore, although traffic on the partially completed canal in 1774 had reached 42,693 tons, by 1778 levels had actually dropped to just 34,077 tons as the canal experienced the effects of a recession brought on by the American War of Independence. Thus the hoped-for revenue did not materialize at once and was very slow to increase.

Despite this shakey start, trade did improve enough for the first dividend of 1 per cent to be paid in 1789. The gross income for that year was £8,230 and net profit was £2,780. The total tonnage carried was 74,312. Of this some 42,379 tons (57 per cent) was coal. The rest consisted of stone (7,569 tons), corn (4,366 tons), lime (3,955 tons), lead (3,862 tons), timber (3,444 tons) and iron (1,544 tons). Other traffic included pottery and beer. The opening of various linking tramways resulted in a steady increase in traffic so that by 1795, the company was able to pay a dividend of 6 per cent. In 1826, 103,000 tons were carried yielding £13,582 in tolls. Among the loads shipped in 1840 was a cargo of Anston stone destined for the new Houses of Parliament.

This modest prosperity continued into the middle of the nineteenth century but the Chesterfield was never to emulate the huge success of some of the canals built at the same time. Perhaps the key drawback was the fact that the line only had one junction with the outside world: at West Stockwith. Over the years there had been numerous suggestions for links with other canals or simple extensions. As early as 1771 Brindley had suggested a canal from Swarkstone on the Trent & Mersey Canal to Chesterfield. Another proposal had a line connecting with the Sheffield Canal that was eventually proposed as part of the Grand Commercial Canal project. This scheme, which would have joined the Peak Forest, Sheffield, Chesterfield and Cromford Canals, was proposed in 1824 at a cost of £574,130. Also during the 1820s a westward extension to Barlow and Calver was suggested. In 1852 the Sheffield and Chesterfield Junction Canal was proposed. None of these plans came to fruition, and by the 1840s it was all too late anyhow.

The Sheffield and Lincolnshire Junction Railway (from Sheffield to

Gainsborough) was proposed in 1844. In response, the Chesterfield Canal Company formed the Manchester and Lincoln Union Railway in 1845 with a view to converting parts of the canal into railway. Such was the threat that the two companies formed a joint committee and agreed to future amalgamation. Under an Act of 7 August 1846 the M&LUR was authorized to construct a railway from Staveley to the canal at Worksop. The Act also enabled the amalgamation of the railway and the canal as the Manchester and Lincoln Union Railway and Chesterfield and Gainsborough Canal Company, and then to further amalgamate with the S&LJR (by now called the Manchester, Sheffield and Lincolnshire Railway). The canal lease was valued at £147,912 and the Chesterfield company was dissolved. The Manchester and Lincoln Union Railway amalgamated with MS&LR on 9 July 1847. The Act stated that the new company was to keep the canal in good order and to maintain reasonable tolls.

During the course of all the manoeuvring, the canal had become neglected and, in places, difficult to navigate because of subsidence. As a consequence, in 1848 the new company set about a programme of maintenance. This lead to an increase in revenue and even the railway company began to carry goods on the canal. But the scheme to turn part of the canal west of Norwood into a railway was not forgotten. Plans were considered throughout the 1870s and early 1880s but were not progressed. In 1888 the canal still carried 62,075 tons but toll receipts had declined to just £2,793. By 1905 the tonnage had fallen to 45,177 (of which coal comprised 15,408 tons and bricks 11,070 tons) and there were only forty working boats still operating. By now, the length between Staveley and Chesterfield had become unnavigable due to subsidence.

Between 1871 and 1906 some £21,000 had been spent repairing Norwood Tunnel. In 1904 the minimum headroom was down to 4 ft 10 in and although there was an official timetable for boat movement, the relative infrequency of traffic meant that boatmen used the tunnel as they pleased. The final *coup de grâce* for the tunnel came in 1908 when a roof collapse under the Harthill to Kiveton Park road closed the through route. In fact this closure meant that no commercial traffic travelled beyond Shireoaks.

The new century saw a series of amalgamations and absorptions with ownership of the canal passing initially to the Great Central Railway and then, in 1923, to the London & North-Eastern Railway. The new owners continued to maintain what was left of the waterway. The tidal lock at West Stockwith, for example, was enlarged and repaired in 1923–5 and the line was kept free of weed. The Second World War saw a mini-revival in trade with the carriage of munitions and a restored coal-carrying business from Shireoaks colliery basin. After the war this coal trade stopped and the carrying of bricks from a factory at Walkeringham ceased in 1955. In 1961 it was proposed to close the line and applications to use it for pleasure boating

Tomlinson's yard at Stockwith Basin in the early years of the twentieth century
Ware/The Boat Museum Archive

were refused. The last commercial traffic moved warp (a type of silt from the mouth of the Idle that was used for metal polishing in the cutlery trade) from West Stockwith to Walkeringham in 1962.

The 1950s were, therefore, a rather bleak decade for the Chesterfield Canal, and its future was not bright. The Inland Waterways Protection Society carried out a survey of the line in 1958–9 and rallies were held at Chesterfield and Worksop in order to publicize the plight of the canal. On 24 May 1960 a public meeting was held in Chesterfield to consider the future of the waterway. It was proposed that the line from West Stockwith to Worksop be retained for pleasure boating and that the section up to Kiveton, and from Spinkhill to Chesterfield, be kept as a water supply channel. However, the stretch from Kiveton to Spinkhill was to be infilled and sold. The recommendations were, therefore, somewhat of a curate's egg.

The 1968 Transport Act secured the future of the canal from Worksop to the Trent as a cruiseway but the whole section between Worksop and Chesterfield was allowed to decline and sections have been infilled and even built on. The campaign of the Inland Waterways Association to retain the rest of the waterway was supported by the setting up of the Retford and Worksop (Chesterfield Canal) Boat Club in 1962. The Boat Club and (since 1976) the Chesterfield Canal Society have continued to lobby for the restoration of the line beyond Worksop. Volunteers have made a start and the first lock (No. 1 at Lockoford Lane) was restored in April 1990. The key problems for the restorers will be the reopening of the Norwood Tunnel and re-routeing of the line around Killamarsh where houses have been built on the original course. The hope is that the Chesterfield will once again be fully navigable within the early years of the new century.

The Walk

Start:	Norwood Tunnel – eastern portal (OS ref: SK 500825)
Finish:	Worksop railway station (OS ref: SK 585798)
Distance:	7 miles/11 km
Map:	OS Landranger 120 (Mansfield & The Dukeries)
Outward:	British Rail Worksop to Kiverton Park (enquiries: (0522) 539502)
Car park:	At Worksop station
Public transport:	British Rail Worksop

Leave Kiveton Park station and walk towards the signal box. Turn right to reach the canal. Don't go immediately to the towpath but follow the advice of a public footpath sign and walk along a dirt track which leads to an entrance to a factory (right). Go straight on following some overhead power cables. The path goes over a canal feeder and on through grassland, initially to the right and then to the left of the power cables. Eventually the path

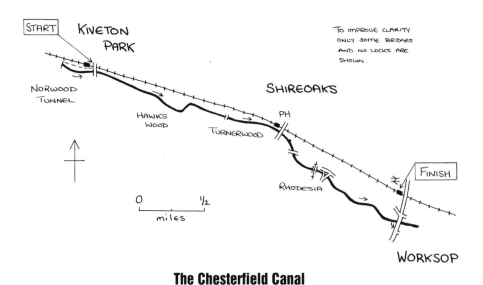

The Chesterfield Canal

splits and a left-hand branch goes down and over the entrance to Norwood Tunnel so that you are now facing back to the station and walking on the right-hand bank of the canal.

Norwood Tunnel is 2,850 yd long and took just four years to build. It was officially opened on 9 May 1775 and was closed in 1908 following a roof collapse about 1/4 mile from this, the eastern, portal. It is actually a relatively shallow tunnel and many authors have suggested that later engineers, such as Thomas Telford, may well have built most of it as a cutting. The big problem for the canal society is, of course, how to restore it. Although very firmly bricked up, I'm told that this end is regularly inspected and is in good condition. The western end however has been plugged at a point where the M1 goes over the top. Much of the ground in between consists of coal reserves and it has been proposed that restoration of the tunnel could be undertaken in conjunction with the mining industry. Recent developments in that business may, however, rule that out for some time.

The towpath along the first half-mile of the canal was being cleared when I made my visit here and it was a hive of activity. While the weeds and brushwood were being cleared, classes of biology students were studying the burgeoning wildlife. Half-way along this first stretch back to Kiveton Park station, the feeder crossed earlier enters the canal. The water comes from the Harthill and Pebley Pond reservoirs which are 2 miles to the south-west near Harthill. The feeder canal, the Broad Bridge Dike, is marked on OS Landranger 120. These reservoirs were built in 1806, nearly thirty years after the canal had opened, in order to overcome what was becoming an embarrassing shortage of water in this, the summit, pound.

At the first bridge, Dog Kennel Bridge, the towpath changes sides and we continue under two bridges with Hawkswood now dominating the scene to the right. After a further bridge (Pudding Dike Bridge), the canal swings left and then right to reach a bridge and the start of the Thorpe flight of locks. There are fifteen of them altogether although many are presently only barely discernible and part of the excitement of the next half a mile or so is to see if your lock tally matches the official number. The trick is to recognize the two triple staircase locks and the two double staircase locks. For those unfamiliar with a staircase lock, it is one in which the top gate of one lock acts as the bottom gate of the next. Easy if the lock-gates are in position, harder when the locks are as dilapidated as this. The key is to look for the recesses for the lock-gates along the sides of the lock chamber. As a clue, the sequence goes: a triple, three singles, a triple, a single, a double, a single and a double. While attempting to recognize the locks, the canal passes through some wonderfully evocative woodland. The expanded lagoons between the locks add to the mystery of the place.

The Thorpe Locks end at Turnerwood where there is a small hamlet and an old quarry basin. After this we continue past the Turnerwood flight of seven locks. After the fourth, the Brancliffe feeder from the River Ryton enters the canal. After the seventh, we go under a bridge and cross an aqueduct (over the River Ryton which marks the border between South Yorkshire and Nottinghamshire) before arriving at Shireoaks. Cricket fans can sit here awhile to watch the game in the canalside Steetley Sports Ground (one batsman hit a rather fine straight six on my visit). Those who aren't fans can walk up to the road bridge to visit The Station pub (Shireoaks station is to the left) or the small shop to the right. The road bridge has been culverted and will need rebuilding before the canal can be restored above this point.

Continue by crossing the road and taking the steps on the other side back down to the towpath. After a short distance the path goes over a roving bridge which marks the entrance to the old colliery basin. Coal traffic continued here until the Second World War and it is hoped that it may be busy again some day although this time as a marina. Our route now continues past a lock and a much rebuilt lock-keeper's cottage and on past two more locks to the outskirts of Rhodesia. After a road bridge, a lock and a rail bridge, we enter the centre of the village where the canal survives going under the new A57 fly-over only to be culverted under two road bridges. At the first of the two, the towpath changes sides to the right-hand bank. We are now heading into the outskirts of Worksop and we pass Deep Lock, a bridge and then Stret Lock and a road bridge. This is shortly followed by what remains of the Lady Lee arm on the southern (towpath) side. An otherwise incomprehensibly positioned roving bridge still crosses the old channel. This branch formerly led to the Lady Lee Quarries half a mile to the south-west.

From here it is only a short distance to the last of the derelict locks, Morse Lock, and the head of the navigation. After passing a winding hole that marks the site of the Inland Waterways Association's 1988 Worksop Water Festival, the canal and towpath suddenly have a much more well-kempt appearance. The large area of water to the left here is Sandhill Lake; a flooded quarry that is now used for fishing and watersports. The centre of Worksop is now quite close and after passing our second canalside cricket ground (this one is used periodically by Nottinghamshire), we arrive at the former site of Worksop wharf – now a car park. In its heyday it was lined with warehouses and maltings and boats carried coal in and malt out. On the other bank was the Shireoaks Colliery Company coal wharf. The walk ends at Town Lock. Here there is a commemorative stone erected in 1977 to celebrate the canal's bicentenary.

It isn't possible to walk on past the lock. The land on the other side of the bridge is used by British Waterways as a depot and it is they who have blocked the towpath from here on. To complete the walk, therefore, we have to return to the car park and walk around the perimeter of a DIY shop to the road and turn left. If you cross the road and look on to the BW depot, you will see a rather fine old warehouse that bestrides the canal. This was formerly owned by Pickfords who at one time was an important canal carrying

Worksop Town Lock is
wedged between the shops in
the centre of town

company. They only later turned to road haulage. The canal society's book-let reports that on the undersurface of the warehouse arch are trapdoors through which goods were lifted or lowered from and to waiting boats. To complete the walk, continue along Carlton Road where the railway station can be found a few hundred yards along on the left.

Further Explorations

The whole of the extant Chesterfield Canal is open to walkers and those armed with an Ordnance Survey map should be able to navigate themselves along the entire 32 miles from Norwood Tunnel. With readily available public transport, the 11 mile section between Worksop and Retford makes for a quiet (apart from a length that runs parallel with the A1 near Ranby) afternoon stroll. Starting at the Retford end, take the A638 road to Newark and cross the canal at the Carolgate Bridge. Turn right to walk along the right-hand bank. The Chequers Inn at Ranby (roughly 6 miles) makes a good resting point. The towpath changes sides just before Osberton Lock (the first out of Ranby) and then changes back again two bridges further on at Manton Turnover Bridge. Should you prefer to divide the walk, East Midlands bus no. 42 (enquiries: (0909) 47577) stops at the Chequers Inn.

A shorter walk (about 2¹/₂ miles) that is chock-full of interest starts at West Stockwith (OS Landranger 112, ref: SK 790947) on the banks of the River Trent. For those without a car, Retford & District bus no. 96 runs to the village from Gainsborough. For those with a car, park in the small car park opposite the White Hart Inn. Walk back to the road and turn left to cross the River Idle. Even before the Chesterfield Canal, West Stockwith was an important port for Chesterfield and east Derbyshire traffic. Prior to the canal, goods were shipped overland to Bawtry, then on to the River Idle and along to Stockwith where it was transhipped on to the vessels that plied the Trent. The village has thus been a busy and relatively prosperous place since the fourteenth century, as the fine houses on the eastern bank suggest.

Walk up the track to the left of both the river and its massive vertically lifting floodgate. Our way goes up on to the flood banks and on to the second barrier where there is a drainage pumping station for the surrounding low-lying agricultural land. The path follows the river around a series of bends and then goes through a gate near the old pumping station at Misterton Soss. This rather fine old building (it dates from the 1830s) used to pump water up from the Mother Drain, a collecting channel for the many criss-crossing drains that service the surrounding countryside.

Just past the pumphouse, take the road left which goes past a kennels, bends around to go under a railway bridge and bends left to reach Misterton and a bridge over the Chesterfield Canal. Here on the right is Misterton Bottom Lock and, beyond Station Road Bridge, Misterton Top Lock. Return to the start of the bridge and walk along the left-hand bank of the canal and past (or via) the Packet Inn. The straight section of canal runs under the railway and on for half a mile. When you reach a bridge, go up to the road (near the Water Boat Inn) and cross both it and the canal to go down some steps to the right-hand side of West Stockwith Basin.

Today the basin is a popular mooring place for pleasure boats but it was once the loading and unloading site for the vessels from the canal and the barges and keels that worked the Trent. West Stockwith Lock, the route to the River Trent, can be seen on the eastern side of the basin. The building to the left of the lock-houses is the lock-keeper's office and on the right is an

West Stockwith Basin in 1992

old warehouse (the date 1789 is enscribed on the wall facing the river). At one time there was also a stables and a blacksmith's shop.

Walk past the warehouse building and cross the Trent-side gate of the lock. Just on the right, in front of the lock-keeper's house, is a winch which was used to pull boats on the river into the lock. Continue walking along the embankment of the Trent with the basin now to the left. This path soon reaches the road, the bridge over the Idle and the car park.

Further Information

The Chesterfield Canal Society says that 'nothing less than full restoration of navigation to Chesterfield' will satisfy it. It'll be a big job but a worthy one and those who wish to help should contact:

> The Chesterfield Canal Society,
> 30 Park View,
> Kiveton Park,
> Sheffield S31 8SE.

The society publishes two very useful booklets which will expand on the information already provided in this chapter. The first is a brief history entitled *The Chesterfield Canal*; the second a towpath guide entitled *The Chesterfield Canal (West Stockwith to Rhodesia)*.

A more substantial volume on the Chesterfield is:

Roffey, James, *The Chesterfield Canal*. Barracuda Books, 1969.

4
THE FOSSDYKE NAVIGATION
Saxilby to Lincoln

Introduction

Although we are all familiar with the long, straight Roman roads that criss-cross the country, it is perhaps less well known that the Romans also made much use of water transport. In Lincolnshire it is actually possible to see and walk along a Roman canal! The Fossdyke can arguably be called the oldest artificial line of inland navigation in England; built fifteen centuries before the Exeter Canal and sixteen before the Sankey Brook. And those with a sense of rightness in these things will be glad to know that it's pretty straight.

At its western end, the Fossdyke Navigation forms a junction with the River Trent at Torksey, about 16 miles downstream of Newark. From there the line heads east, through Torksey Lock to Drinsey Nook where it meets the A57. After passing through Saxilby, the Fossdyke heads on under the shadow of Lincoln Cathedral until it reaches Brayford Pool and the junction with the River Witham, 11 miles from the Trent.

The broad, flat landscape of Lincolnshire isn't to every walker's taste – one boating guide I've read describes it as boring – but the fine prospect of the cathedral and the delightful river front in central Lincoln should be sufficient reward for anyone venturing forth.

History

The town of Lindum was established in AD 48 by the Roman IXth legion at the junction of Ermine Street (which went north) and the Fosse Way (which went south-west to Exeter). It was an important strategic position and the town grew rapidly, encouraged by the surrounding rich agricultural land. Although the roads were clearly of great importance to the Roman occupants for the movement of troops, the inward shipment of bulk materials was always going to be more of a problem. In addition, it would clearly have been an advantage to have used the productive Lincolnshire soils as a source of provisions for the garrisons further north. Thus the Roman mind turned to the potential of water transport.

There are two artificial canals in Lincolnshire which are generally accepted as being of Roman origin. They form just part of an extensive Roman waterway system which, although probably originally built for drainage purposes, provides through communication from the Cambridge area as far north as York. The Car Dyke is 56 miles long and runs from the River Nene east of Peterborough to the River Witham, a few miles below Lincoln. The 11 mile long Fossdyke (or Foss Dyke or Fossdike or Fosdig) connects the Witham with the Trent at Torksey. It is generally accepted that both canals were built as a way of connecting the farming area of the fens with the military garrisons of the north. But, although the Cambridgeshire Car Dyke has been shown to date from Roman times, there is no absolute proof that these artificial waterways in Lincolnshire are Roman. All that can be demonstrated is that they are pre-Norman and from then on archaeologists have had to conject and surmise. Car Dyke has been tentatively dated at AD 60–120 and as such it has been suggested that it formed part of Emperor Hadrian's period of imperial planning. Although the dating of Fossdyke has proved more difficult, a bronze statuette of Mars was found at Torksey during dredging in 1774 and an inscribed sepulchral tablet was found at Saxilby. These finds have lent weight to the theory.

Both dykes were probably built by simply digging out the earth from a relatively easy terrain and throwing it up to form banks on either side. There is certainly no suggestion that the construction of the navigation would have presented any great feat of engineering even though both lines pass through low-lying land liable to flooding. When the canal engineer John Rennie saw Car Dyke he said that 'a more judicious and well-laid out work I have never seen'. No doubt part of the route used the course of rivers. On the Fossdyke, for example, the builders were able to use (albeit with some straightening) the line of the River Till for the first 4 miles west from Lincoln. The overall width of both dykes was approximately 100 ft although the navigable line was probably only about 30 ft. Archaeologists have suggested that the line was plied by barges similar to those that are seen on relief sculptures of the time.

The position of Lincoln on this system of internal waterways was almost certainly responsible for the prosperity of the town during Roman times and it became a kind of inland port. The remains of a Roman quay, for example, were found during the construction work on the telephone exchange at the corner of Broadgate and Rumbold Street. All the way along, the town's river front must have been furnished with quays for the large volume of trade that was handled. Lincoln certainly became an important transhipment port for grain going north. The dyke would also have been used for local traffic. Excavations at Littleborough have revealed 'colour-cooked wares' from the Nene valley, near Peterborough, that were almost certainly brought by water. Roman pottery kilns are known to have been built along the Fossdyke, for example at the racecourse in Lincoln and at Little London near Torksey. The proximity of the waterway may suggest that finished pots were shipped to market using the waterway network.

What happened to the dykes during the Dark Ages remains unclear. It is, however, generally considered that when the Danes invaded in the 870s, they overran Lincolnshire by the simple expedient of sailing down the Humber, the Trent and then along the Fossdyke into Lincoln itself. From then it isn't until 1121 that the navigation again appears in the history books. Symeon of Durham records that the Fossdyke was reopened for traffic following dredging work carried out for Henry I. How long the line had been closed is unknown although it was possible that it had become unnavigable at the time of the Norman invasion. The line must certainly have been navigable in the reign of Henry II as a small Cistercian nunnery was built on its banks near Torksey at that time. The house became an object of benevolence for the trading community, a point perhaps enhanced by the fact that the nunnery was dedicated to St Nicholas, the patron saint of sailors.

Between the twelfth and fourteenth centuries the Fossdyke carried the wool of the Midland counties to Lincoln for export to Flanders. In later days it carried corn, wool and malt to the West Riding, Yorkshire, returning with linseed cake, manure, coal and manufactured goods. In 1319 a trip from Lincoln to York took two days. All this activity spurred the growth of the town of Torksey which was able to exploit its position at the junction with the Trent. It is said that some of the inhabitants sought to exploit the situation rather unfairly. In the thirteenth century Robert of Dunham (a village on the Trent above Torksey), who was a bailiff for William of Valence, was levying a toll of a half penny for every ship that passed from Lincoln along the Fossdyke to Dunham. This action was probably illegal but obviously highly profitable. The records suggest that 160 ships a year did the voyage.

By the middle of the fourteenth century the line was beginning to decline and wool was being carried by road. The dyke was becoming seriously silted and in July 1335 a petition of complaint was sent to the king. He responded by setting up a commission to survey the dyke and to clear it. It appears that contractors were being paid to maintain the waterway but they weren't doing so. Although the situation was remedied, problems continued off and on for nearly two centuries. In 1518 the Bishop of Lincoln, William Atwater, was appointed commissioner and he stimulated interest and managed to start a fund-raising scheme. But on his death in 1521 the plan faltered and was quickly forgotten. The dyke languished in ill-repair for over a century. The situation was so bad that the state of the navigation was recorded in poetry by John Taylor (1580–1653). The poem, 'A very merrie wherry-ferry voyage' describes the Fossdyke as a 'ditch of weeds and mud' and records that a single stretch of 8 miles took 'nine long hours'.

In the early years of the eighteenth century, Lincoln council was struggling to maintain the navigation which had been vested to them under an Act of 1671. Revenue was enough to pay for minor works but it was clear that a major dredging effort was needed which was estimated to cost £3,000. Although a one-third share on the line had been sold to James Humberton in 1672, he was unable to assist and the council sought external help. This was found in the shape of Richard Ellison (of Thorne in the East Riding, Yorkshire). It was agreed that Ellison would maintain the channel to a depth of 3 ft 6 inches in return for a rent of £75 p.a. (£50 to the council, £25 to Humberton). The deal was sealed on 18 September 1740 and the revamped line was opened in 1744.

The reopening of the waterway helped restore Lincoln from the period of decay into which it had deteriorated since the sixteenth century. This revival is mirrored by the steadily increasing toll receipts along the Fossdyke: from just £700 in 1751 to £1,499 in 1774 to £5,908 in 1814. By 1805 there was a horse-drawn packet-boat that plied the line to York. By now the dyke had become a major conduit for wool en route via the Trent, the Humber, the Ouse and the Aire & Calder Navigation to the towns of the West Riding. The line also carried away corn, ale and pit props with the town receiving coal in return.

The lease on the dyke passed down the Ellison family over the years and, it has to be said, that they tended to enjoy the income without any particular inclination to maintain the line. In 1836 Richard Ellison IV became the owner of the lease at a time when income had risen dramatically, from £5,000 in 1813 to £8,000 in 1825; a situation no doubt aided by the gradual development of the rest of the country's canal system. The development of the trade at this time is no better illustrated than by the fact that some 40,000 tons of corn, harvested p.a. in Lincolnshire, was being shipped via the Calder & Hebble Navigation and the Rochdale Canal to feed the cotton workers of Lancashire. However, with this growth in traffic was a concomitant growth in complaints about the condition of the navigation. Again it was said that the Ellison family were creaming off the profits with no view to improve the line.

The Fossdyke meanwhile was silting up and legal battles followed in which many complainants sought to wrestle control of the waterway back into public control. The Lincolnshire farmers were producing and the merchants handling a steadily increasing volume of goods for despatch to

Yorkshire and Lancashire and it's no wonder they were concerned about their main route to market. The trade was largely in the hands of merchants whose yards and warehouses flanked the Brayford Pool. By 1836 it was said that the condition of the Fossdyke was so bad that a trip from Hull to Lincoln took as long as one from England to the United States, i.e. three weeks. The bridge at Torksey was a major impediment as vessels could not get under it when the Trent was high. The canal channel was reported to be too shallow and shoals near Saxilby meant that vessels with half a cargo had to discharge into lighters. Linseed cake and coal were becoming scarce in Lincoln. It is perhaps understandable that things were getting heated. A compromise bill in which it was proposed to make the navigation capable of drawing 5–6 ft of water was drawn up. The plan was to spend £40–50,000, shared equally between Ellison and public funds, to improve the line. However, the scheme was lost in a wave of ill-feeling. In 1839 Ellison, perhaps eager to rid himself of a headache, offered to sell his lease to the council for £16,000 but they resolved that the price was too high particularly as a railway to Gainsborough could be built for less.

Thus Richard Ellison IV set about improvements under his own steam. The whole line was dredged and the stretch from Drinsey Nook to Torksey widened. By this time 40,000 tons of coal p.a. were being delivered from the Nottingham coalfield. In return, the quays of Brayford Pool exported wheat, barley and flour to Manchester, cattle to Rotherham and Manchester, and wool to the West Riding. In return came hardware, cotton goods, earthenware, linen, woollens, timber, linseed cake and oil.

The first rumblings of railway competition were heard in 1825 when a line from London to Cambridge with extensions to Lincoln and York was proposed. It wasn't forthcoming immediately and not until 1846 did the Lincoln & Nottingham Railway provide a route to the Midlands. This was followed in 1848 by the Manchester, Sheffield & Lincoln Railway which connected the city with Lancashire and the West Riding. Ellison clearly can't have thought too long about ridding himself of his heirloom. On 21 December 1846 he granted a 894 year sublease to the Great Northern Railway at a rent equal to his net revenue plus 5 per cent, namely £9,570 p.a. Although the council and businessmen of Lincoln were alert to the dangers of monopoly, the railway soon made its market by capturing both the passenger and the freight traffic. By 1852 the packet-boats which regularly plied the waterway were gone. Freight traffic between 1848 and 1868 dropped by 70 per cent. Although the Great Northern was officially obliged to maintain the waterway, Fossdyke was gradually being more and more neglected and the channel steadily silted up. In 1854, for example, it took one boat owner 6 hours to drag his boat from the Pyewipe Inn into Brayford Pool (a distance of a little over a mile). Although some minor dredging was carried out, the situation did not improve very much. Despite this, water

Brayford Pool in the early 1900s

The Boat Museum Archive

transport still had its protagonists and barges still served the Brayford Pool. At the time a boat from Lincoln to Hull took 24 hours compared with the train which took 30 hours and cost more.

By the turn of the twentieth century Fossdyke was still carrying more than 75,000 tons of cargo p.a., including timber, agricultural produce and general merchandise. Perhaps the key factor in the continuing use of the line was the fact that most of the works in Lincoln still had river frontage. The main problem for the carrying companies was that there was not a constant water depth of 5 ft; an issue that didn't concern the railway company particularly.

Although by the First World War the navigation was declining, the use of the channel as a drain was still important and there was some traffic. In 1914 William Franklin Rawnsley, in *Highways and Byways in Lincolnshire*, states that the view of Lincoln Minster from Saxilby with 'the sails of barges in the foreground as they slowly make their way to the wharves . . . is most picturesque'. The barges in use at this time were 'low, round-nosed . . . with widespread canvas'. Even in 1949 Arthur Mee in *King's England* describes the barges making their way along the Fossdyke. Today the commercial traffic has gone but full use is made of the waterway by leisure cruisers who follow the route once taken by the Roman legions.

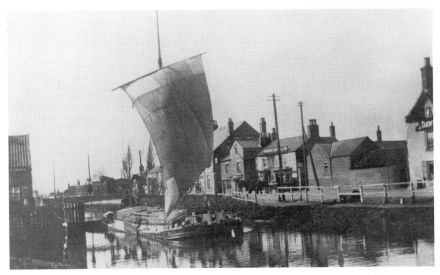

Keel under sail at Saxilby in 1930

W.E.R. Hallgarth/Ware/The Boat Museum Archive

The Walk

Start:	Saxilby railway station (OS ref: SK 892752)
Finish:	Lincoln railway station (OS ref: SK 975709)
Distance:	6¹/₂ miles/10 km
Map:	OS Landranger 121 (Lincoln)
Return:	British Rail Lincoln to Saxilby (enquiries: (0522) 539502)
Car park:	At Saxilby station
Public transport:	British Rail Lincoln

This is a pleasant stroll but there is a length of road walking (albeit on a pavement) at the beginning that may deter some. One possible way to avoid this is to take the Roadcar bus no. 352 (enquiries: (0522) 532424) which runs from Lincoln to Gainsborough. Some drivers may be prepared to stop at the Broxholme turning thereby avoiding the stretch along the road.

From Saxilby station, walk out to the High Street and turn right to go past the post office. Continue into Bridge Street where the Fossdyke appears on the right. Walk past The Ship and The Sun Inn. Just before a road bridge, bear right up a slope to the A57 Gainsborough Road. Continue over a junction where the A57 now becomes the Lincoln Road. Continue along the

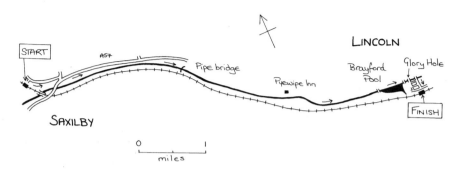

The Fossdyke Navigation

pavement until you pass the turn off for Broxholme. Cross to the opposite side of the road and go over the River Till which enters the Fossdyke from the left. Just after the crash barrier, a footpath sign points along the left-hand embankment of the dyke.

After the traumas of the road, the solitude of the dyke gradually takes over and it gets quieter and quieter until you feel that you're about to come to a dead stop. After rounding a bend and passing a high pipe bridge, the lofty position of the embankment allows fine views of Lincoln Cathedral in the distance. By now there's only the herons and the fishermen, both of whom sit down by the dyke staring mournfully at the waters. The banks here appear solid but they are apparently made of sand, occasionally quicksand, and in former times were a constant headache to lessee Richard Ellison who found that they often collapsed. This was particularly the case after a vessel had run against them.

The land to either side of the dyke here was always susceptible to flooding and before the nineteenth century was inevitably under water. In 1804 John Rennie was called in to advise and, under a scheme known as the Lincoln West Drainage, an area of 4,000 acres was drained. By 1806 the plan was complete and one local correspondent is said to have reported that 'fat beef was growing on Swanpool where fishes lately swam'. The scheme was undertaken partly by the construction of an embankment and partly by the insertion of catchwater drains to intercept upland water.

Two miles from the road, the line bears left and then goes under the new flyover that forms part of the Lincoln ring road. About a hundred yards further on we pass the canalside Pyewipe Inn (Chef & Brewer). Charles Hadfield suggests that the name Pyewipe derives from peewit – that is the lapwing. The dyke passes over an aqueduct (which crosses a drainage dyke). The Fossdyke then, unusually, meanders slightly before reaching the outskirts of Lincoln. The first signs of this are the golf course to the left and then the British Waterways depot (the East Midlands Navigation Lincoln office) to the right. By now the towpath has broadened to a dirt track.

The path reaches a road (Fossbank). Continue close to the dyke along a pedestrian alleyway to reach an electric lift bridge which marks the entrance to Brayford Pool. Continue along a cobbled alley to a road. Bear right to go past the home of the Lincoln Boat Club and Bunnys Wine Barge. This leads to a pedestrianized area from where there are good views across the pool to the river disappearing over in the far right corner. In medieval times, the bulk of what is now Brayford Pool (and then known as Bradeford) was simply a marsh with a ford across it. The area was probably first used as a quay in Roman times. But until the eighteenth century Brayford had been a pool of mud and sand without wharves on its banks, surrounded by gardens and orchards. With the passage of the Horncastle Act in 1792 (see Further Explorations), trade was improved. Gardens were turned into coal-yards or covered with warehouses and the pool quickly became a port. By 1810 the pool could admit vessels of 50 tons alongside the quay and was no longer dry in summer. Today it is a popular spot for cruising boats who are warned that, although wide, it is rather shallow away from the dredged through channel that runs along this side.

The walk now passes the Royal William IV pub; a fine place to sit outside on a warm summer's lunch-time. If not stopping, continue past the stop gates and under the road bridge to walk by the side of the River Witham. Until a bridge was built by Richard Ellison here in 1801, the only way

Brayford Pool in 1992

pedestrians could cross was via a series of stepping stones and then only in summer. This path leads round the backs of some big high-street stores and winds around a solicitors building along North Witham Bank to reach the most famous waterway sight in the area: the Lincoln High Bridge and the Glory Hole.

The Glory Hole is a single, vaulted arch that is 22 ft wide. It was originally built in the twelfth century although the buildings that sit atop it date from the sixteenth century. When the Horncastle & Tattershall Canal Act was passed in 1792, the possibility for boats going from the Brayford Basin through the Glory Hole and on to the River Witham was increased. However, at that time, the channel was too shallow to allow such traffic to pass. Goods were off-loaded on one side of the bridge, transported by land to the other side and reloaded. The H&TC Act therefore enabled the new company, together with the Witham and Sleaford Navigations, to deepen

The Glory Hole in central Lincoln

the channel under the bridge to 3 ft 6 in. This was done in 1797 and the cost shared between the interested parties.

The path now goes up some steps to the left to reach the pedestrianized shopping centre. Continue down the other side and walk on along Waterside North; a pleasant city waterway which is surely a model for others. Cross the River Witham at a footbridge and walk straight on (i.e. turn right from the tow-path course) and along Sincil Street to reach the railway station.

Further Explorations

The Horncastle & Tattershall Canal runs for 11 miles from the small market town of Horncastle south to a junction with the River Witham. The Tattershall Canal was originally a separate entity. It was built in 1786 by John Gibson and John Dyson and ran for about a mile from the River Witham at Tattershall Ferry to the village. The new scheme for a line to Horncastle owed a considerable amount to a local dignitary, the botanist Sir Joseph Banks, who saw the benefits that would accrue to the town if it had a route to export its agricultural produce and for the import of salt, coal and other heavy goods. The canalization of the River Bain was enabled by the Horncastle Navigation Company Act passed on 11 June 1792. This Act enabled the new company to buy the Tattershall Canal as well as to deepen the channel under the Lincoln High Bridge (see above).

William Jessop surveyed the line but did not become involved in its construction. This was a pity as the building of the canal was dogged by a string of incompetent engineers. By the time the line was opened to Dalderby (2½ miles south of Horncastle) in 1797, the company had run out of money and this remained the terminus for the next five years. Further funds were raised following an Act in 1800. This allowed John Rennie to plot a new, straighter course to Horncastle and the line was fully opened on 17 September 1802. It had cost £45,000, four times Jessop's original estimate. In all there were twelve locks (measuring between 71 and 75 ft long and 15 ft wide) and a fall of 84 ft to the Witham. The completion of the canal made Horncastle into a mini boom town. The traditional agricultural businesses (such as wool merchants) expanded greatly and many new ones, such as the manufacture of farm implements, traders in artificial manures and coal merchants, were started. The Horncastle Gas Light and Coke Co. was also able to open in 1833. From 1826 a steam packet passenger service was operating from Horncastle to Lincoln and Boston.

Up to 1812 profits from the line were used to pay off the not inconsiderable debt, but by 1813 trading showed a credit of nearly £1,000 and a dividend of 5 per cent was issued. Dividends varied between 5 and 7 per cent from then until 1856. In the early 1850s the canal was moving nearly 10,000 tons of coal a year into Horncastle and taking just over 5,000 tons of corn, wool and other goods back on to the Witham.

In 1848 the Great Northern Railway's line from Lincoln to Boston was opened and a branch to Horncastle was completed in 1854. The canal company responded by reducing its tolls so that receipts stayed at roughly £850 p.a. during the first decade of railway competition. But trade gradually declined and the last dividend of $1^1/2$ per cent was paid in 1873. An attempt to spruce up the line during the late 1870s was not very successful and in 1889 the local council proposed to close it. This was done on 23 September 1889. Despite this, coal was still being shipped in to Coningsby in 1910. Norman Clarke reports that the line could easily be restored for use by pleasure boats if only the spirit were willing.

It is possible to walk along various stretches of the canal and there is a fascinating short stroll of about $2^1/2$ miles from the centre of Horncastle. The town is on the Lincoln to Skegness A158 on OS Landranger 122 (Skegness) at ref: TF 258695. There are a number of small car parks near the Market Square. Alternatively Roadcar bus no. 6 goes to Horncastle from Lincoln (enquiries: (0522) 532424).

From Market Square turn left to walk along High Street and then right along Bull Ring. Before this road reaches the A158, turn right along Wharf Road with the canalized River Waring to the left. This is the site of the old Horncastle Canal South Basin. Continue along Wharf Road until the canal goes under the, comparatively new, road bridge. Cross the main road at the pedestrian lights and then turn right to walk along the grassy left-hand bank of the canal. The path goes over the South Ings Drain. The drain was built to straighten the rather convoluted course of the Old River Bain which it joins about a mile to the south. The sluice (or staunch as it is called) was used to control the level of water in the canal. The path passes in front of the swimming pool and then on to a footbridge that goes over the course of the canal which bends left here to start its line to the River Witham. The swimming pool was originally a dry-dock that was owned by the navigation company. It was sold and converted into a pool in 1875. Near here is a comparatively recent weir. For the full walk, turn left to walk down the left-hand bank. This route takes you past the site of Horncastle Lock. At the first bridge (near Thornton Lodge Farm), cross and return on the opposite bank (following the course of the old railway line and now the Viking Way). This returns you to the other side of the footbridge where you will meet those who didn't do the full walk and who have merely crossed the bridge and turned right.

The path now follows the course of the River Bain and heads north to the North Basin. We cannot follow it but have to walk out to a road. Turn right to pass the Maypole House School to reach the Lincoln road. Cross this and go along West Street. Bear right into Bridge Street where the road crosses the River Bain. The road leads back to Market Square. Before jumping in the car, turn left past the post office to go along St Lawrence Street. This leads to the site of the old North Basin opposite Watermill Road. The wharf is now a car park. Apart from the watermill, the basin here was surrounded by two windmills, and malt kilns. There was also a tannery and currier's workshop, a boot and shoe factory, a saddler, a basket maker's, coal merchants, cutlers, gasfitters, ironmongers and steel merchants, a chandler, a nail maker, a blacksmith, a coachbuilder, a pipe maker, a glover, and a plumber. Perhaps the most vigorous business down here, however, was the beerhouse and brothel run by a Mr Daft.

Further Information

There is no Fossdyke society as such but the Inland Waterways Association has a Lincoln & South Humberside branch. For further information contact the London office (see Appendix B).

The history of the Fossdyke is described in:

Boyes, J. and Russell, R., *The Canals of Eastern England*. David & Charles, 1977.

For information on the Horncastle & Tattershall Canal:

J. Norman Clarke, *The Horncastle & Tattershall Canal*. The Oakwood Press, 1990.

5
THE HUDDERSFIELD CANALS
Mirfield to Marsden

Introduction

While the Sir John Ramsden's Canal to Huddersfield was a minor and high-ly sensible arm of the Calder & Hebble Navigation, the Huddersfield Narrow Canal was a bold and almost reckless endeavour. It attempted to scale the Pennines head-on: rising 436 ft from Huddersfield via forty-two locks in just under 8 miles and burrowing through the Pennine Hills along the longest canal tunnel ever built in Britain. This is the kind of stuff that great adventures, if not great profits, are made of.

Sir John Ramsden's Canal forms a junction with the Calder & Hebble Navigation at Cooper's Bridge between Mirfield and Brighouse. From there, it runs for 3³/₄ miles to Aspley Basin in Huddersfield. The SJRC and the Huddersfield Narrow Canal form a junction, in theory at least, near Huddersfield University. The HNC then starts its 19³/₄ mile route over the Pennines to Ashton-under-Lyne. En route it passes through Milnsbridge and Slaithwaite before reaching Marsden and the Standedge Tunnel. Exactly 3 miles 418 yd further south-west, the line re-emerges from the hill at Diggle and starts its downward trek through Greenfield and Mossley to reach Stalybridge where it has been infilled and built over. The final stretch begins on the other side of town and continues for just a mile and a half to Ashton-under-Lyne where the canal meets the Peak Forest and Ashton Canals at Portland Basin.

The Tame Valley is highly industrialized but is always pleasant and/or interesting and is often both. It also has the carrot of leading on to the wide-open spaces of the central Pennines. This means that, even without boats, it's one of the finest towpath walks around.

History

The Act which enabled construction of the Calder & Hebble Navigation received its Royal Assent in June 1758. By 1774, 21^1/$_2$ miles of river from the Aire & Calder Navigation at Wakefield to Sowerby Bridge were open for traffic via twenty-seven locks each measuring 57 ft 6 in by 14 ft 3 in. With this important waterway from the east coast into the mill town of Halifax in place, it wasn't too long before the prospects for a navigable line to Huddersfield came under consideration.

The first mention of a branch canal to Huddersfield was made in the C&HN Act of 1758. In 1766 Robert Whitworth surveyed a line of 3^3/$_4$ miles from Cooper's Bridge (about 1^1/$_2$ miles west of Mirfield) to King's Mill, Huddersfield and several petitions to Parliament followed without success. By 1773 the major local landowners, the Ramsden family headed by a still under-age Sir John Ramsden, sponsored another survey, this time by Luke Holt and John Atkinson. In the bill, promoted by the trustees of Sir John in 1774, it was claimed that the canal would benefit Huddersfield through the cheaper import of raw materials. But, as Charles Hadfield points out, the Ramsdens owned virtually the whole of Huddersfield at that time and the family must have seen the venture as a safe, and potentially highly lucrative, investment. The Act, for what was to become known as Sir John Ramsden's Canal (but which is also known as the Huddersfield Broad Canal), received its Royal Assent on 9 March 1774. The Act proposed a line of nine locks built to take Yorkshire keels measuring 57 ft 6 in long by 14 ft 2 in wide. The cost was estimated at £8,000. Tolls were set at 8d. a ton for coal, lime and stone, and 1s. 6d. a ton for other goods.

The canal, which opened in the autumn of 1776 at a cost of £11,974, was a modest success from the off. Huddersfield was becoming an important wool-spinning town and was growing rapidly. The SJRC thus became an important conduit for the export of its products as well as for the import of raw materials. The canal carried textiles, coal, lime, stone, timber, wool, corn, glass and other goods. To cope with this, new docks, wharves, and warehouses were built at Aspley Basin in Huddersfield where there were also a number of hostels built for the canal workers.

Meanwhile, on the western side of the Pennines, the Ashton Canal had been built from a basin at Ducie Street, Manchester to Ashton-under-Lyne. This project had been authorized by Parliament in June 1792 and it wasn't too long before it was realized that if the SJRC and the Ashton Canal were linked, the result would be the shortest water route between the east and west coasts. A group of Ashton Canal shareholders began to consider the idea in May 1793 and, following a survey by Nicholas Brown, Benjamin

Outram proposed a line at a cost of £178,748. On 4 April 1794 the Act was passed to enable the construction of a narrow canal (to save both water and costs) of 19¾ miles by seventy-four locks from the Ashton Canal via Marsden to the SJRC at Huddersfield. The most significant engineering work on the line was to be a tunnel through Standedge – a distance of 3 miles 176 yd (later extended). The Act authorized share capital of £184,000 and provided powers to raise a further £90,000 if it was needed.

Construction work started in July with Benjamin Outram as engineer. By November 1796 the line was open from Ashton to Stalybridge and from Huddersfield to Slaithwaite and, presumably, some toll income was being received. However, the difficulties of building the Standedge Tunnel were already becoming evident and by 1798 it was becoming increasingly hard to find a contractor willing to take the job on. The situation was not helped by tenuous finances and the fact that some sections were so poorly constructed that they had to be rebuilt. When Robert Whitworth acted as deputy to Outram during the latter's illness, he described the masonry and earthworks as the worst of any he had seen.

By 1799 the canal was virtually complete with the northern length from the tunnel to Huddersfield, and the line from Ashton to Saddleworth, finished. But only 20 per cent of the tunnel was complete. With finances exhausted, the company tried to raise £20,000 by mortgage but only succeeded in raising £8,000. Further actions from the company brought in some additional funds but it was still short. Serious floods in 1799 didn't help and another £7,000 was needed to undertake repairs. The situation was remedied by an Act in 1800 which enabled the company to raise an additional £20 on each share already issued. The tunnel was still a major headache. At one stage it was thought that a railway should be built across Standedge to link the two ends of the canal, but this idea was rejected as impracticable. By June 1801 only 1,000 yd of the tunnel were cut with another 1,000 yd only partially bored. The company's financial problems had been partly solved when it raised £48,190 by the issue of new shares but the tunnel remained unopened.

Meanwhile one John Rooth had started a small carrying business on the western side of the tunnel and by April 1801 he had been made superintendent for the canal. By October, with Outram having resigned, he was given the additional responsibility for the tunnelling work which was proceeding, if slowly, from each end. The work was paid for by the creation of further new shares in 1804 and then by calls of £16 on all shares in 1806. These actions raised a further £125,914. In 1806 Thomas Telford was called in to survey the work to date and to make recommendations on how to proceed. With his plan and the additional funding, the company was able to complete the line. Although the company's bankers and the Diggle reservoir were both broke during the course of 1810, December of that year saw the tunnel

Workmen repairing a breach on the Huddersfield Canal at Golcar, probably at the turn of the nineteenth century

Ware/The Boat Museum Archive

finally finished. It was (and is) the longest canal tunnel in Britain and cost a total of £123,804 against Outram's estimate of £54,187.

The grand opening of the Huddersfield Narrow Canal (and hence the Huddersfield trans-Pennine route from Manchester to Hull) occurred on 4 April 1811. The completed canal was just under 20 miles long and comprised some seventy-three locks built to the narrow boat gauge of 72 ft by 7 ft. The canal had five aqueducts: Stalybridge, Royal George (Greenfield), Saddleworth, Scarbottom and Paddock. It had ten reservoirs, four of which held more than fifty million gallons: Haigh, Slaithwaite, Red Brook and Swellands. The total cost was £273,463.

Unfortunately trade did not come to the HNC either as freely or as fast as anticipated. In 1816 the canal was described as 'a bad speculation for the subscribers and . . . a warning to others how they engage in such tremendous works'. The key problem was that by 1811 the Rochdale Canal had already established itself and was cheaper to use. In 1813, for example, traffic along the HNC totalled 40,460 tons compared with the Rochdale's 290,508 tons. This competition forced the combined HNC, SJRC and Ashton Canal to reduce their tolls. In addition, a plan to charge 1s. 6d. to pass through Standedge Tunnel was dropped. The situation was not helped by the fact that the HNC had been built to Brindley's narrow boat gauge as used on the Ashton and Peak Forest Canals to the south. The classic narrow boat was, however, too long for either the SJRC or the Aire & Calder Navigation both of which took barges (Yorkshire keels) measuring 57 ft 6 in by 14 ft 2 in. As a consequence cargo had to be transhipped at Huddersfield. To overcome this problem a number of short narrow boats were constructed, able to work both lines as well as the waterways in the Calder Valley. Their success, however, was always going to be limited given their reduced cargo-carrying capacity. Attempts by the HNC to convince the Aire & Calder to make its locks longer were never successful. The HNC were similarly unsuccessful in convincing the Rochdale to join with it to fix prices. This predicament was not helped by the problems with the water supply (the canal was often closed because of drought) and a new reservoir capacity had to be built. On top of all this, maintenance of the HNC was expensive and there was criticism of bad workmanship on the locks. This forced the company into a further round of building and repair.

Despite the difficulties, trade into the 1820s grew gradually so that by 1822 receipts were £12,284. Cargo included coal, corn, lime and limestone as well as general merchandise. The towns along the route, like Marsden, Slaithwaite and Milnsbridge benefited from the canal as did the many mills along the valley. In the following years the company appeared to have much

Lock at Holme Mill, Slaithwaite, in the early years of the twentieth century

Ware/The Boat Museum Archive

to do but still the money did not come in to pay off the capital invested, and it wasn't until 1824 that the shareholders received their first dividend of £1 per share. Even so this did not mean an end to the company's money problems and authority was given to borrow up to £10,000 to promote trade. Five unfruitful years followed during which a new warehouse in Manchester was built and reservoir capacity expanded. As a consequence no dividends were paid until 1831 which again saw £1 per share.

Trade continued to increase slowly and in 1833 a dividend of £1 10s. was paid, rising to £2 in 1837–9. But in 1835 both the HNC and the SJRC attended a meeting with the Aire & Calder, the Calder & Hebble, the Rochdale Canal Company and the Ashton Canal Company to discuss the coming of railway competition. Some tolls were cut but in many ways this was a phoney war. By 1838 the company was forced to reduce its tolls in the face of direct competition from the Manchester & Leeds Railway and the battle began in earnest. Although the committee was able to pay a dividend of £2 in 1841, by 1842 it was unable to pay anything. Tolls of £2,435 in 1841 had dropped to £1,720 in 1842. Further toll cuts were implemented in 1843 followed by economies of £2,000 a year but this still failed to raise enough trade.

In 1844 the Huddersfield & Manchester Railway was promoted for a line from Stalybridge to Cooper's Bridge, a route that ran almost parallel to the combined HNC and SJRC. The HNC committee who had been asked to recommend a new plan for the company was quick to take the hint. It soon reached agreement with the H&MR for amalgamation. Following the passage of the necessary Act on 21 July 1845, the new Huddersfield & Manchester Railway & Canal Company paid £183,730 for the HNC and £46,560 for the SJRC. The canal was a valuable asset to the railway company. Standedge Tunnel, for example, was used extensively during the building of a new rail tunnel to move spoil as well as for ventilation and drainage.

Unlike many canals which operated in direct competition with a parallel railway, the HNC/SJRC worked (at least in theory) in co-ordination with its younger neighbour. However, in 1847 both the railway and the canal were leased in perpetuity to the London & North Western Railway. The LNWR's enthusiasm for the canal was somewhat less overt. The year after it was absorbed by the LNWR, the SJRC had carried 120,207 tons, but from then on through traffic declined. There was a brief revival in 1856 when the Aire & Calder tried to rebuild a carrying trade to Manchester via Huddersfield but, generally, cross-Pennine trade, and hence that on the HNC, evaporated. Local traffic on the SJRC held up comparatively well with eighteen to twenty-five boats a day working the waterway in 1863. In addition, the LNWR began to sell canal water. In 1875 the extraction rate was some 200,000 gallons a day.

In the early 1890s, 75,000 tons of cargo a year were being exchanged with the C&HN; three-quarters of which was to and from Huddersfield itself. The cross-Pennine route, however, was flagging. When the canal tunnel closed for repairs during 1892 and 1893, the LNWR shipped the canal cargo by rail and when the tunnel reopened that trade stayed with the railway. The canal to either side, however, remained active. Remarkably enough the HNC carried 161,899 tons in 1898 compared with 169,487 fifty years earlier.

By 1905 the transfer from the C&HN amounted to 53,850 tons to and from Huddersfield with 11,020 tons going on along the HNC. Little of it was reaching the tunnel and traffic over the summit ceased in 1905. Trade on the lower sections of the HNC continued after the First World War but was all but gone by the Second. In 1944 an Act of Parliament was obtained by the London Midland & Scottish Railway (into which the LNWR had been absorbed in 1923) to abandon the line. On 1 January 1945 the C&HN bought the SJRC together with a half-mile length of the HNC for £4,000. The rest was then abandoned. At this time eighty barges a month were carrying power-station coal. As it was now part of the C&HN, the SJRC was nationalized on 1 January 1948.

The last recorded through passage from Ashton to Huddersfield took place in 1948 when the *Ailsa Craig* took Tom Rolt, Robert Aickman and others on what sounds like an eventful journey (the trip is described by Rolt in *Landscape with Canals* (Alan Sutton, 1986)). This famous excursion, which occurred at the very beginning of the canal restoration movement, was only possible by the application of brute force from twelve men supplied by the British Transport Commission who hauled the boat over the shallows. During the course of the trip *Ailsa Craig* sank at least once and became wedged in the then still barely open Standedge Tunnel. The lock-gates on the HNC were removed in the early 1950s and, in October 1953, the coal trade along the SJRC ceased. Although the HNC was considered long gone by the British Transport Commissions' Board of Survey in 1955 and by the Transport Act of 1968, the SJRC was listed as a cruiseway under the 1968 Act. Luckily the channel of the HNC was maintained as a reservoir for local industry and with the formation of the Huddersfield Canal Society in 1974, restoration began. Since then a phenomenal amount of work has been carried out with the objective of seeing cross-Pennine boat traffic by 4 April 2001 at the latest. Perhaps the most encouraging evidence of the success of the venture occurred in 1988, when an Act of Parliament was passed to officially allow boats to navigate the restored lengths of the HNC.

The Walk

Start:	Mirfield railway station (OS ref: SE 203195)
Finish:	Tunnel End, Marsden (OS ref: SE 039119)
Distance:	14^1/$_2$ miles/23 km (or shorter)
Map:	OS Landranger 110 (Sheffield & Huddersfield) plus small portion on 104 (Leeds, Bradford & Harrogate)
Return:	British Rail Marsden (or Huddersfield) to Mirfield. Hourly weekdays, every two hours on Sunday(enquiries: (0484) 545444)
Car park:	Mirfield station (southern side)
Public transport:	British Rail serves Marsden, Huddersfield and Mirfield

With the proximity of the railway for the entire length, this walk can be conveniently divided into two shorter lengths: one along the Sir John Ramsden's Canal from Mirfield to Huddersfield of 6^1/$_2$ miles (10 km) and one along the Narrow Canal of 8 miles (13 km).

Mirfield to Huddersfield

From the car park at Mirfield station, go down the steps and turn right to go under the railway bridge. Within a short distance the road crosses the Calder & Hebble Navigation. Turn left to walk along the right-hand bank.

The C&HN runs from a junction with the Aire & Calder Navigation at Wakefield, for 21^1/$_2$ miles along the Calder Valley to Sowerby Bridge near Halifax. For part of its route it uses the River Calder although some sections consist of artificial cuts which shorten or simplify the line. Built to provide the woollen merchants of Halifax with cheap water transport, the C&HN received its Royal Assent in June 1758 and was open to vessels (measuring 57 ft 6 in by 14 ft) as far as Sowerby Bridge in 1774 at a cost of £75,000. The line was a prosperous one and even when the railways came to the Calder Valley in the 1840s, it continued to be busy. Part of its success was due to the fact that, with the Rochdale Canal at Sowerby and the SJRC at Cooper's Bridge, it formed a component of two of the three cross-Pennine canal routes. A wide range of cargo was carried including coal, wool, stone and foodstuffs. Competition began to have an effect in the 1860s but it was only after the First World War that traffic levels dropped dramatically. Despite this, trade continued until after the Second World War when many

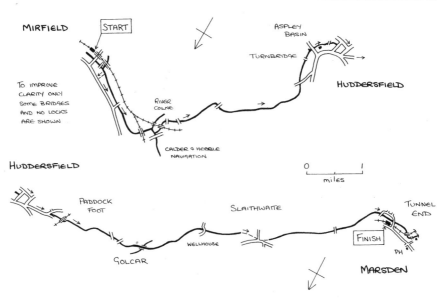

The Huddersfield Canals

barge owners saw a threat from nationalization and either sold up or ceased trading. The last cargo vessel to navigate the full length of the C&HN reached Sowerby Bridge in 1955 while the last into Brighouse ran in the early 1960s. Coal traffic from Wakefield to Thornhill power station, Dewsbury, continued for some time after this. The C&HN was always viewed relatively favourably by the British Transport Commission and was classified as a cruising waterway in the 1968 Transport Act.

The walk starts near a maltsters on the left bank and then soon passes a boatyard, complete with a covered dry-dock. Many hundreds of wooden-hulled Yorkshire keels were built at the Ledgard Bridge yard in years gone by and motor cruisers are now repaired here. The canal engineer William Jessop and contractor John Pinkerton had a dry-dock for many years at Mirfield made out of an old cut they had replaced in 1776.

We leave the Mirfield cut via Ledgard Bridge Flood Lock and Ledgard Bridge itself to meet the River Calder for the first time. After crossing a redundant railway bridge, the towpath ends and we are forced to follow the path round to the A644 Brighouse to Dewsbury road. Turn left and walk on for approximately half a mile. Just after The Pear Tree Inn, turn left into Wood Lane. The first bridge crosses the River Calder and the second goes over the Battyeford cut. Turn right along Waterside Walk and back on to the left-hand bank of the navigation.

This short, quiet section ends at another footbridge and stop lock where

Entrance lock and lock-house at the start of the Sir John Ramsden's Canal

the C&HN and the Calder once again merge. Go straight on to cross the river and turn left to continue along the right-hand bank. This leads to a further artificial cut which appears as a right turn near the first of the Cooper's Bridge Locks. Walk along the cut to reach the next road bridge which is Cooper's Bridge (carrying the A62 Huddersfield–Leeds road). Go up to the road and turn left to cross the cut. A second bridge crosses the river. From this to the left, one can see the start of the SJRC. Take a path on the far side of the bridge that goes left down to the canal. Cross the small bridge and turn right to walk along the left-hand bank of the canal and alongside lock 1 (Cooper's Bridge Lock), the entrance lock from the River Calder. The lock is typical of the SJRC; being a broad lock measuring 57 ft 6 in by 14 ft 2 in. The lock-keeper's cottage still stands on the right.

From here the canal swings left to run parallel with the River Colne (to the left). The route from here to Huddersfield isn't aesthetically pleasing but the curious mixtures of organic solvent smells will keep you constantly at wonder as to what precisely the factories along the way are up to. After bending right, the line goes under the Huddersfield to Leeds railway and on to lock 2 (Colnebridge Lock) and Colnebridge Road Bridge. The view is now dominated by the brick viaduct built in 1910 to carry the Midland Railway extension to Huddersfield. It's a splendidly built structure with some delicate features that wouldn't shame a garden wall. Sadly it hasn't seen active service since the track was lifted in 1937. After the viaduct a short stretch leads to Ladgrave Lock (No. 3) and a dye-works. The Huddersfield Canal Society's booklet points out that the proximity of the bridge at lock 3 limits the length of the balance beams and makes it impossible for the whole length of the lock to be used.

After Longland's Lock (No. 4) the canal goes under a footbridge and then another old railway viaduct; once part of the Huddersfield to Kirkburton line. The canal now bends right under Leeds Road Bridge (A62). Just beyond it is an old mill in which the loading doors have been converted into windows. There are now extensive playing fields opening up the view to the left and the first sight of Huddersfield ahead. Turnpike Road Lock (No. 5) is quickly followed by Riding (or Riddings) Lock (No. 6) and Fieldhouse Green Lock (No. 7) which has Fieldhouse Lane across its lock tail bridge. After passing the 2 mile post, another short pound brings us to Falls Lock (No. 8) and then Red Doles Lock (No. 9) with its lock tail bridge, lock cottage and rather dilapidated outbuildings.

We have now reached the summit pound on the SJRC. The line goes under a concrete bridge and past the council incinerator. We then go under the girder bridge which carries Hillhouse Lane and walk on to the next bridge: Turnbridge or Locomotive Bridge. This extraordinary structure, built in 1865, is a lifting bridge. By operating the wheels and chains on the far bank, the bridge deck rises parallel with the waterway. It is called Turnbridge because of the swing bridge that formerly occupied the site.

It is now a short walk into Aspley Basin. The basin was originally the terminus of the SJRC and was later the transhipment basin for cargo undertaking the full cross-Pennine route; the narrow boats of the HNC being too long for the locks of the SJRC and the Yorkshire keels being too wide for the locks of the HNC. The basin was equipped with numerous wharves, cranes, mills and warehouses and must have been a busy spot. Indeed, the basin was still receiving coal into the 1950s. Many of the original buildings have been flattened; the most notable clearances occurring in 1963 when the Wakefield Road was widened. There are some (barely) surviving original buildings and a basin. There is also, for those contemplating the full walk to Marsden, Ramsden's Landing Restaurant and PJ's Café Wine Bar.

The line of the canal now continues under the busy Wakefield Road ahead. To reach it, turn left to walk past the café/wine bar and on to St Andrew's Road. Turn right and then right again along Wakefield Road. After 100 yd, turn right to go down some steps and under the road. The path now leads to the environs of Huddersfield University. Almost immediately on the right is a former transhipment warehouse. It was built in 1778 for Sir John Ramsden and used for wool storage. Next to the warehouse is a crane which consists of a cast-iron base with a wooden jib. There is another crane sited further towards the main university building. This was once positioned on a small canal arm which looped around to the right.

Walk on along the path in between the buildings and over the Shore Mill Goit which feeds the SJRC with water from the River Colne. Shortly the line bends sharp left to a culverted bridge which, now, separates the SJRC from its narrow sister and, apparently, houses the university's sewer. Beyond this, the SJRC originally went straight on across Firth Street to join the Colne near Kings Mill. The HNC, however, bends right to the first narrow lock: Stanley Dawson Lock (1E – where E stands for east of the Standedge Tunnel). The lock and the following stretch of canal are enclosed by the surrounding mills to form a kind of dank chasm through which the HNC attempts to find a path. In fact these mills provided the final traffic for the canal with the last load of coal being delivered to the wharf above the lock in the early 1950s. The wharf can be picked out by the stone setts and what remains of the mooring rings. After Coal Wharf Lock (2E) is another coal wharf serving the adjacent Priestroyd Mill and then Queen Street South Bridge which still bears the Ramsden coat of arms. From here the canal is

The first lock on the
Huddersfield Narrow
Canal in Huddersfield

completely blocked by a 'new' building. In restoring the HNC, the canal society hopes to burrow underneath. To do this the line will have to be lowered by shifting lock 2 to the other side of the tunnel.

To continue the walk or to complete this stretch to Huddersfield, turn left and then right along Colne Road. Turn right into Chapel Hill. Go up the hill, over the line of the canal and on to a major road junction. If continuing the walk, turn left to go along the Manchester Road – signposted A62 to Oldham. If completing the walk here, go straight on into the pedestrianized town centre (New Street). Walk on for about 1/4 mile and turn left into Westgate and then second right into Railway Street. Huddersfield railway station is on the left.

Huddersfield to Tunnel End, Marsden

If starting from Huddersfield railway station, walk on to Railway Street and turn right to Westgate. Turn left and then right along New Street. This pedestrianized street soon arrives at a major road. Bear half right along the Manchester Road – signposted A62 to Oldham – here you will meet those who are continuing from Mirfield.

The second half of the walk starts along the A62 from where the canal can be seen wending its way through the factories in the valley to the left. Eventually the road crosses the canal at Longroyd Bridge. Longroyd Bridge Lock (4E) can be seen on the right-hand side. To reach the towpath, walk around to the left of some buildings into a car-spares garage and then right to reach the canal. On the right is the lock. Turn left to walk along the left bank. Continue round a bend and under a railway viaduct (the Huddersfield to Penistone line). Beyond the viaduct the canal turns sharply to Paddock Foot Lock (5E) and then, almost immediately, Paddock Foot Aqueduct. The positioning here is most unusual with the lock by-wash weir starting in the middle of the aqueduct span. The buildings beyond the aqueduct are part of an iron foundry while across the canal is a boilermakers. This is closely followed by Mark Bottom Bridge.

Stoney Battery Road Bridge has been replaced by an embankment and the canal culverted. Shortly we pass Mark Bottom Lock (6E) and arrive at Fountain Lock (7E), the first of the flight of five that proceeds through the mills of Milnsbridge. Contrarily a notice on the wall of one factory overlooking the canal states that bathing is prohibited. As this option is thus excluded, we carry on along the next stretch and past locks 8E and 9E (Roller and Isis Locks). Market Street/Whitely Street Bridge is then followed by Spring Garden (10E) and Library (11E) Locks. After Morely Lane Bridge we pass lock 12E (Rough Holme Lock) with its small lock hut, and the canal crosses the River Colne via Golcar Aqueduct. Shortly thereafter is a rare sighting for the HNC of Golcar (or Holme Mills) Swing Bridge.

By the time we reach locks 13E/14E (the Ramsden Locks), we feel that we are entering into true Pennine scenery and finally beginning to leave the old mill buildings behind. Above 14E the towpath forms a causeway between the canal and Ramsden Mills mill-pond. There are sluices into the dam where the canal swings right near the river. Appleyard Bridge is followed by Golcar Brook Lock (15E) and the Westwood Locks (16E and 17E). In 1894 Lowestwood Lane Bridge was widened with iron. After 17E there is a brick lock hut and the remains of a wharf. We pass locks 18E (Can) and 19E (Holme) then Lees Bridge which was originally a swing bridge.

Locks 20E (Spot) and 21E (Waterside) are followed by the village of Slaithwaite where the canal comes to an abrupt, culverted, end. This section of the canal was infilled in 1956 when there was little hope for the line. Luckily nothing has been built on top and the course of the old waterway can still be followed as a path through an area of well-kempt grass. Eventually the path reaches a car park; the boundary of which marks the former site of Pickle Lock (22E). Continue on to the road where there are a small selection of shops. The canal line continues along a grassy border and across a road and a small area of parkland (opposite the Shoulder of Mutton pub) to the tail bridge of lock 23E (Dartmouth Lock). The lock itself has been infilled and now sits underneath a picnic site but just a little further on water has been restored.

The scenery now becomes more wooded. Slaithwaite reservoir, one of ten that served the canal and one of the biggest at 68,200,000 gallons, lies up the hill to the right. After the infilled lock 24E (Shuttle Lock), a road crosses. We pass locks 25E and 26E (Shaker Wood and Skew Bridge Locks) and start our ascent to Marsden. Locks 27E–30E (Mill Pond, Waring Bottom, White Hill – beyond which there is a new road bridge – and Bank Nook) follow. At Booth Lock (31E) a former winding hole can be seen with a canal cottage dating from 1858. The canal then bends to the right and we pass Cellars Clough Mill and go under a footbridge which crosses to the nearby Sandhill cottages. To the right of the next lock (32E – Pig Tail), is Sparth reservoir (8,150,000 gallons) which is, along with Slaithwaite reservoir, one of only two that still supplies the canal with water. Locks 33E–38E (Sparth, Cellars, Moorvale, White Syke, Smudgers and Colne) follow in short order. Ahead we obtain a clear view of the lumpy heaps on the side of Standedge; spoil that was dumped during the excavation of one of the four tunnels that pass through the hill.

The canal now goes under Warehouse Hill Bridge and on to Warehouse Hill Lock (39E). The canal then swings right past an old wharf and some cottages and on through a cutting that is, in fact, made up of a succession of heaps of tunnel spoil. We pass locks 40E and 41E (Hopper and Dirker Locks), go under two bridges and arrive at Marsden railway station and the appropriately named Railway Lock (42E). With this the canal reaches the summit pound which, at 645 ft, is the highest point of any artificial water-way in Britain. There is now just half a mile to Tunnel End. The line goes under a road bridge and on through a narrowed section which was formerly the site of a bridge. We go under the railway to reach an old canal ware-house that is now used as a British Waterways maintenance depot. The warehouse was originally served by its own canal arm and was used when this was the terminus for the eastern length of the canal. Cargo was tran-shipped onto pack-horses and carts for road transport over Standedge. In the warehouse wall can be seen the top of the arch of a former covered boat dock. From the towpath, at the head of the winding hole, can be seen the two single and the double railway tunnels with the stepped outfall of Tunnel End reservoir (22,650,000 gallons).

Follow the path round and across the final bridge to reach Tunnel End and the Tunnel End cottages. These were built in the 1840s to house the tunnel-keepers who guarded the comings and goings through the hillside. The cot-tages now house the Canal and Countryside Centre which has an exhibition on the canal and sells books and leaflets. Beyond the cottages is the entrance to Standedge Tunnel which at 5,456 yd long (extended to 5,698 yd after the rail-way was built) (4,950 and 5,209 metres respectively) is the longest canal tunnel ever built in Britain. It must also be one of the deepest as in places it is over 600 ft below the surface of Standedge. Only portions of the tunnel are lined and, in those parts that are not, the rock surface is very rugged and rough with the dimensions varying considerably: sometimes just 7 ft by 7 ft and at others opening out into a sizeable cavern. The tunnel took sixteen years to build and cost £123,804 – roughly 40 per cent of the total cost of the HNC. It was finally opened on 4 April 1811 when 'upwards of five hundred people' passed through singing 'Rule Britannia' and other patriotic songs.

There is no towpath. Boats were 'legged' through by men who lay on their backs and walked the vessel along. Given the wide variations in the bore of the tunnel, it must have been a difficult job and it isn't surprising that the passage of a fully laden boat took four hours. Boats were admitted according to a strict schedule. They were allowed to enter the west end between 6 and 8 a.m. and 5 and 8 p.m., and the eastern between 12 and 2, day and night. Boatmen could measure their passage using cast-iron dis-tance plaques set in the roof at every 50 yd. In 1816, in order to speed things up a bit, the company considered using a steam tug. After much thought, and some experimentation, a tug service was introduced in 1824. This was, however, abandoned in 1833 in favour of more efficiently orga-nized leggers. Subsequently, the engineer John Raistrick suggested the cre-ation of an artificial current through the tunnel although this was never tried. The tunnel was closed in 1944 due to rock falls and subsidence but the HC Society are confident that the channel can be restored albeit after the expenditure of several million pounds.

Although the canal tunnel was the first through Standedge, it wasn't the last as there are no fewer than three railway tunnels. The first (a single-line tunnel) was opened in 1849 to house the Huddersfield & Manchester Railway & Canal Company line. It took just three years to build; a job made much easier by the fact that the canal tunnel was already in place. A second single-line tunnel was opened in 1871. The final tunnel is the double-track tunnel used today. This was completed in 1894.

To return to Huddersfield or Mirfield, retrace your steps to the railway station next to lock 42E.

Further Explorations

The Ashton end of the HNC is open for walking from Stalybridge to the western end of Standedge Tunnel. For a walk of 4$^1/_2$ miles, park the car near Greenfield railway station – which can be found on the A669 Holmfirth–Oldham road (OS Landranger 109, ref: SD 992047) – and take the train to Stalybridge (enquiries: (0484) 545444).

Leave Stalybridge station and turn right to go under the railway. Bear right along Market Street to pass the Staveleigh Medical Centre and an open bus station. Continue past The Talbot and turn right into Melbourne Street. This road crosses the River Tame and becomes pedestrianized. Some 50 yd after The Friendship pub, the road goes over a bridge without apparently crossing anything. This marks the spot where the HNC once went through central Stalybridge on its way to a junction with the Ashton Canal at Ashton-under-Lyne (to the right). Turn left here to walk into Armentieres Square car park. The canal originally crossed the square to go to the right of the parish church ahead. Our route takes us along Corporation Street to the left of the church. The canal originally took a course through the Delta Crompton Cables Factory on the right. At the end of Corporation Street turn right into Mottram Road. About 200 yd along, go past a left turn and walk on for a further 100 yd to some greenery and a noticeboard that announces 'The Tame Valley'. Turn left. It is unlikely that the section of the HNC through Stalybridge will ever be restored. As an alternative the canal society have proposed to build a new navigable line along the River Tame which follows a similar course to the canal albeit slightly to the north of the original route. The eastern end of this diversion will rejoin the original route near the site of a disused railway viaduct.

The first lock along the now extant, if a little overgrown, canal is the infilled 7W. From here the line of the waterway winds its way through the outskirts of Stalybridge to a point where the aforementioned old railway bridge crosses the waterway. The new line of the canal, the Stalybridge bypass, will leave from here. We, meanwhile, continue onwards to another infilled section with an electricity substation on the left. The route wends its way underneath an electricity pylon and then, a couple of hundred yards further on, passes over the site of lock 8W (Bywith Lock), indicated by a slight rise in the ground level. A short distance on and the canal is once again in water although the next bridge (a former swing bridge) has been culverted. Just beyond the bridge was the site of Hartshead power station of which only the landscape scars and a tall, partly demolished, conveyor bridge remain.

Keep walking and you will finally reach the restored section at Black Rock Lock (9W). This is shortly followed by Avenue Lock, Terrace Lock (10W and 11W) and the 220 yd Scout Tunnel. A towpath goes through the tunnel but those who suffer from claustrophobia or who have small children may prefer to take the path that passes over the top. The tunnel is brick-lined for the first few yards and then cuts through solid rock. Whitehead's Lock (12W) will cause some problems in restoration as there has been some ground movement locally which has resulted in the whole structure becoming twisted. Above the lock, the canal becomes increasingly more of a refuse tip but improves after a road bridge and Wharf Cottage Lock (13W) where the canal is dominated by the large red edifice of Mittan Mill and the stone-built Woodend Mill. This is Mossley. Here the line swings right to Woodend Lock (14W) and the towpath changes sides to the left-hand bank.

The canal bends left to Roaches Lock (15W) near a pub of the same name. After a road bridge we reach Gas Works Lock (16W) where we recross to the right bank via the tail bridge. After Division Lock (17W) the canal goes under Division Bridge (formerly the Lancashire and Yorkshire boundary) and crosses the River Tame via the stone-arched Royal George Aqueduct. The Royal George is the largest of the seven aqueducts on the canal and has been concrete-lined to help stop leakages. We have now reached the outskirts of Greenfield. The canal goes through Keith Jackson Lock (18W), under a road bridge and on to Royal George Lock (19W). The path then rises to a road at the curiously named Well-i-Hole Bridge, under which the canal is culverted. Turn left and go up the hill. Greenfield station is at the top on the left.

Further Information

The Huddersfield Canal Society looks after the interests of both the narrow canal and Sir John Ramsden's. Together with BW and the local authorities, the society hopes to reopen the line in 2001. It can be contacted at:

Huddersfield Canal Society,
239 Mossley Road,
Ashton-under-Lyne,
Lancashire OL6 6LN.

The society publishes a towpath guide and the Kirklees Metropolitan Council publishes an excellent Information Pack about the canals. Both are available at the Tunnel End Canal and Countryside Centre.

For more historical detail the SJRC is covered in:

Hadfield, Charles, *The Canals of Yorkshire and North East England*, Vols. I and II. David & Charles, 1972.

The HNC meanwhile is covered in:

Hadfield, C. and Biddle, G., *The Canals of North West England*, Vol. II. David & Charles, 1970.

6
THE LANCASTER CANAL
Lancaster to Glasson

Introduction

Although a waterway link to the south was planned, and a section (now part of the Leeds & Liverpool) actually built, the Lancaster Canal was never physically joined to the rest of the canal system. Instead the company opted for a 5 mile long railed way from Preston to (what is now) the L&L at Walton Summit (near Whittle-le-Woods). Despite this isolation, the line was so successful that it actually took a lease on its rival railway company. It's worth visiting for that piece of effrontery alone.

The present course of the Lancaster starts in Preston and heads west to Salwick before turning north to Garstang. At Galgate the Glasson arm runs west to Glasson Dock and the Irish Sea. The main line, meanwhile, continues north to Lancaster. On the northern outskirts of the town, the canal crosses the River Lune via one of the most famous aqueducts in the land. The route now runs parallel with the coast to go through Hest Bank to Carnforth. The small village of Tewitfield marks the northernmost limit of current navigation. The closed section north of here plays cat and mouse with the M6 for a while before heading west to go through Hincaster Tunnel. Although dry, the canal can still be traced from Hincaster all the way into Kendal.

The Lancaster Canal stands gloriously alone. Isolated from the rest of the English canal system, it has a kind of proud aloofness and seems none the worse for it.

History

Plans for a navigable line to link the Leeds & Liverpool Canal with the towns of Lancaster and Kendal had been in the wind since the 1760s.

Indeed, in November 1771, a meeting at Lancaster Town Hall had called for a survey of a suitable line. Robert Whitworth carried out two, of what turned out to be several, surveys but none seem to satisfy the would-be promoters and the scheme was dropped. Further plans for a waterway were aired during the 1780s, all of which evaporated in waves of indecision and faltering enthusiasm.

By 1791 the nation was entering into a period which was to become known as canal mania and the people of the north-west were not able to escape the craze. On 4 June 1791 a group of businessmen from Lancaster petitioned for a canal to link the town with the rest of the canal network. A meeting on 8 June resolved to promote a canal and by October, John Rennie was carrying out a survey. Rennie's plan, described to a meeting on 7 February 1792, was for a 75^1/$_2$ mile long broad canal which started at Westhoughton (in the middle of the Wigan and Bolton coalfields). From there the line would go north to Clayton Green and then pass down thirty-two locks to an aqueduct over the River Ribble to Preston. After Garstang the line would cross the River Wyre via an aqueduct to Lancaster, Tewitfield and Kendal. There were to be branches to Duxbury and Warton Crag (near Tewitfield). At this time the southernmost junction with the rest of the canal network was still a matter of debate; the choice being to join either the Bridgewater Canal or the Manchester, Bolton & Bury. With this issue still in limbo, the meeting resolved unanimously to proceed and nearly a quarter of a million pounds was raised on the spot. The Lancaster Canal Act was passed on 25 June 1792. The company was authorized to raise £414,000 with an extra £200,000 if needed. John Rennie was appointed as chief engineer with Archibald Millar as resident. A further branch to a sea dock at Glasson was enabled by an Act of 10 May 1793.

With the construction work underway in early 1793 (John Pinkerton, among others, taking one of the contracts), John Rennie set about finding himself a southern terminus. An early agreement with the Duke of Bridgewater to form a junction with his canal at Worsley fell through. This was then followed by an agreement with the Leeds & Liverpool Canal Company in which it was resolved to form a junction between the two lines at Heapey. Meanwhile the construction of the canal proceeded apace, albeit with recriminations for poor workmanship by both Pinkerton's men and those of a local contractor John Murray. By 1795 the company took control of the undertaking itself with Archibald Miller supervising the works more closely. In order to do this, Henry Eastburn was made resident engineer for the section south of the Ribble.

By 1795 a stretch of 4 miles, from Bark Hill to Adlington (now part of the L&L near Chorley), was opened and the first coal traffic was moving in July 1796. By 2 November 1797 the length from Preston to Tewitfield was opened with a modest celebration which included the firing of guns in front

The barge *Zion* SS taking a party along the Lancaster Canal to Sedgwick
Ware/The Boat Museum Archive

of Lancaster town hall. South of Preston, a continuous line from Bark Hill to Johnson's Hillock (near Whittle-le-Woods) was completed in 1799. The problem that now faced the company was how to join the two ends of its line over the River Ribble. The cost of building a line with locks descending to and ascending from an aqueduct over the river was estimated by the new resident engineer, William Cartwright, at £180,945. A tramroad way, however, was estimated at £60,000 and it was this that was built. Thus, the northern section of the Lancaster was never connected to the southern and has hence always remained separated from the rest of the canal network.

An Act of 1800 enabled the raising of a further £200,000 which paid off the company's outstanding debt and funded the new tramroad. Although there was talk of an alternative route along an extended Douglas Navigation (see Chapter 7), the tramroad scheme was supported by John Rennie and William Jessop and work started. The route involved building a canal/rail interchange basin at the Walton summit (near Whittle-le-Woods) and another in Preston, together with a tunnel through Whittle Hill. The tramroad, which was powered by stationary steam engines, was opened on 19 January 1804.

The company was now able to operate over the majority of its new line and its financial prospects improved enormously. Revenue of just £4,853 in 1803 (for which a $1/2$ per cent dividend was issued) was nearly doubled in

1804. In 1805 a dividend of 1 per cent was paid. At that time the northern end of the navigation remained at Tewitfield and the company still had to complete its route into Kendal. There had been a suggestion for a tramroad but, despite the cheaper cost, this was rejected. The company opted for a canal line and the work proceeded. Meanwhile, even by 1810, the southern end of the canal was still not connected to the rest of the canal network. However, the Leeds & Liverpool were by then pushing to complete their cross-Pennine route between Blackburn and Wigan and an agreement between the two companies was forged. The L&L would use the Lancaster between Johnson's Hillock and Bark Hill from where the L&L would build a short connecting line to Wigan.

With constant delay, due to the impact of the Napoleonic Wars and a repeated lack of funds, the full route, including the Hincaster Tunnel, wasn't open until 18 June 1819. On what must have been a memorable occasion, an audience of 10,000 celebrated on Castle Hill, Kendal. The town's bells were rung and 120 dignitaries consumed a splendid dinner in the town hall. The Lancaster Canal opened twenty-seven years after it was started at an approximate cost of £600,000.

Even before the line was open it was doing relatively well. In 1817 income was regularly in excess of £19,000 p.a. although the dividend was pegged at 1 per cent. Once the full route was open, however, the line really began to flourish. The small town of Kendal, for example, went through a mini-boom period. This increased prosperity was shared by the canal whose income grew by about a third almost immediately. Revenue in the year 1823 was £28,874, with income coming roughly equally from the two ends of the line.

A panoramic view of Kendal, thought to be at the end of the nineteenth century, shows the canal terminus and docks

Ware/The Boat Museum Archive

The volume of traffic carried, however, was more disparate. Of the total cargo of 459,000 tons in 1825, 303,000 tons were moved on the southern line (including the tramroad) and 156,000 tons on the northern. Most of the traffic on the southern line, some 71 per cent, was coal. Despite the growing level of trade, dividends were pegged at 1 per cent until 1825. In 1826, with the Glasson branch opened for traffic, the company was able to raise its dividend to $1^1/_2$ per cent. With the failure of its bankers and increased lending rates on its outstanding loans, however, the company reverted to a more prudent 1 per cent from 1828 onwards.

This, albeit comparatively modest, success of the Lancaster was not to last for long. In 1831 Parliament passed an Act which authorized the construction of the Wigan & Preston Railway. The new line was to follow the course of the Lancaster Canal for virtually the entire way. The canal company realized its vulnerability, particularly in respect of the now outdated tramroad section that linked its two watery halves. A number of schemes were proposed varying from abandoning the entire line south of Preston to amalgamating with the new competitor. One option, that of converting the tramroad into a locomotive-powered railway, was considered in more depth. George Stephenson was asked to look into the possibility and returned with an estimate of £11,895. However, the company was sceptical about the practicality of the scheme.

Meanwhile the Wigan & Preston (now known as the North Union Railway) opened for business in 1834 and another line, that from Bolton to Preston, followed shortly thereafter. With this, the Lancaster reached an agreement in January 1837 in which the railway company would lease the canal's tramroad for £8,000 p.a. and build a new canal/rail interchange basin in Preston. The deal was a bad one for the railway, who, just a year and a half later, obtained an Act which allowed it to use the North Union's line into Preston. Thus the Bolton & Preston Railway found itself paying a lease for a line it didn't need. Although a reduced lease rate of £7,000 was later agreed, the canal company appears to have been unenthusiastic about cancelling the agreement.

By 1836 the canal's revenue had risen to £33,000 p.a. with 550,000 tons of cargo being moved along the line. As a result, the dividend in 1837 was increased to $1^1/_4$ per cent. In 1840 trade was still improving, despite the railway, and income stood at £34,200. But shortly thereafter it was agreed that the tramroad should be closed and the canal company abandoned trade south of Preston. Instead it concentrated on expanding the coal business along the northern waterway, supplied by the railway companies to the Preston terminus and exported via Glasson Dock.

In 1837 competition for the northern traffic arrived with a bill for the Lancaster & Preston Junction Railway. The new line would share a station with the North Union in Preston and would follow the canal north. By June

1840 the railway was open to Lancaster and it may be supposed that the good days for the Lancaster Canal were over. The canal company, however, came out fighting. It halved its passenger fares; an act which enabled it to maintain the numbers who used the route. In addition, the new railway fell out with the North Union and a delay in the building of the Bolton & Preston Railway meant that trade was less brisk than predicted. Thus by 1842 it was the railway company that was in dire financial straits and, contrary to most of the railway-canal competitions, it was the canal company that took a lease on the railway. The deal was one in which the Lancaster was to pay £13,300 p.a. (equivalent to a 4 per cent dividend) lease plus the interest payments on the railway company's outstanding loan. The lease was to last twenty-one years. This arrangement was enabled by an Act of 3 April 1843. Very quickly it appears that the canal company began to exploit the situation. Cargo-carrying became a monopoly and the company was able to cream off relatively high profit levels. Passenger train fares were increased sharply and, at one point, all the seats in third class were removed so that more passengers could be fitted in. Meanwhile the Lancaster & Carlisle Railway was going ahead. An Act was passed in June 1844. The L&PJR, viewing the possibility of a better deal, extracted itself from the Lancaster lease and, instead, leased itself to the new L&CR; an agreement that came into effect on 1 September 1846. The canal company did not surrender its legal control of the railway willingly. Although requested to hand over the line on 1 July 1846, it refused and sought legal action to support its case. The L&CR ignored this and ran its trains to Preston as if it were the lessee and refused to pay any tolls for doing so. Although negotiations were started, the canal company refused to pay its rent in 1848 and each company commenced legal action against the other. At one stage it looked as if the argument may subside when the canal company came close to selling itself to L&CR but this fell through.

After a fatal accident on 21 August 1848, the companies were instructed to sort the matter out by the Railway Commissioners and this they duly did. On 13 November it was resolved that the canal company was to be paid £55,551 (a sum decided following arbitration) for the unexpired portion of the lease. The canal company then gave up control of the line on 1 August 1849. Overall, the deal meant that the Lancaster had made a profit of nearly £70,000 from its railway lease; a sum which allowed it to pay off its debts, pay a dividend bonus of nearly 2 per cent and still have funds for contingencies. This must have been welcome to the shareholders of a company who, even at its peak in 1846, was still only able to pay a 2$^1/_2$ per cent dividend.

In 1850 the new cordiality between the canal company and the railways was cemented when the canal agreed with the L&CR to share business. The canal company was to take the coal and heavy goods traffic (plus that to Glasson Docks) in return for giving up its passenger and general merchandise trade. Although the company had offered to sell its southern end to the Leeds & Liverpool in 1845, the deal that was eventually reached in 1850 meant that the L&L leased the merchandise tolls at £4,335 p.a. for a period of twenty-one years.

The 1850s saw the canal company starting its own coastal trade with five steamers. It also leased its own quay in Belfast. In 1857, perhaps more significantly for the long term future of the canal, the London & North Western Railway was expanding its interests in the north-west and took control of the L&CR. All traffic agreements appear to have come to a close almost immediately, and trade along the Lancaster went into terminal decline. By 1860 the company was seeking to sell itself to the LNWR and in 1864 it succeeded. The Lancaster Canal Transfer Act, passed on 29 July 1864, enabled the LNWR to lease the northern end of the canal in perpetuity for £12,665 p.a. The southern end was leased to the Leeds & Liverpool Canal for £7,075 p.a. By this time the northern half of the tramroad had declined and was now closed. The southern half (Walton Summit to Bamber Bridge), which still had some remaining traffic, was eventually closed in 1879.

In 1885 the LNWR offered to buy the canal company at a price equivalent to £43 15s. per share. The shareholders agreed and the canal was sold on 1 July 1885. The Lancaster Canal Company was finally dissolved on 1 January 1886. In the early years of the LNWR's ownership, the line continued to carry coal along the main line, and various goods, such as grain, minerals and timber, from Glasson. In 1889 the line carried 165,005 tons of cargo and had an income of £18,728. By the turn of the century traffic was dwindling. Cargo loads were down to 130,396 tons and income to £13,984.

In 1944 the London, Midland & Scottish Railway (into which the LNWR had been incorporated in 1923) proposed to close the Lancaster; a move that was defeated by a consortium of local interests. However, by then the trade north of Lancaster was restricted to coal deliveries to Kendal gasworks, a total of 7,500 tons p.a. This business was moved to road transport in the autumn of 1944. The final cargo from Preston to Lancaster was moved in 1947 to Storey's Mill, White Cross, Lancaster. The canal was nationalized in 1948 and, like so many of the nation's waterways, its future looked bleak. The 1955 Board of Survey report for the British Transport Commission placed the canal in category 3: waterways having insufficient commercial prospects to justify their retention. While this was not put into immediate effect, the line from Stainton (near Hincaster Tunnel) was closed and the top 2 miles into Kendal infilled. In 1964 a section in Preston was also filled and a number of other sections were flattened or allowed to decay. In 1968, as a final indignity, the M6 was built across a culverted canal in three places. The northern section above Tewitfield was then sealed by the construction of the A6070.

In 1963, when the future of the canal looked at its bleakest, a group of enthusiasts formed the Lancaster Canal Trust (as the Association for the Restoration of the Lancaster Canal). Since then they have vigorously fought to keep the canal in water and to reopen the closed sections. The situation was certainly improved (if not resolved) when the Transport Act of 1968 listed most of the line as a cruiseway. The year 1990 saw the formation of the Northern Reaches Restoration Group and a reinvigoration of the scheme to re-establish the waterway in full. The isolation of the northern stretch above Tewitfield will not be ended until either the motorway is raised or the canal lowered. A feasibility study by a group of consultant engineers has suggested that this could cost £17.5 million, so it may be some time before Kendal sees boat traffic. But where there's life . . .

The Walk

Start:	Lancaster (OS ref: SD 473617)
Finish:	Glasson Dock (OS ref: SD 445562)
Distance:	9 miles/14 km
Maps:	OS Landranger 97 (Kendal & Morecambe) and 102 (Preston & Blackpool)
Return:	Lancaster City Transport or Ribble Buses nos. 86, 88 and 89 operate from Glasson Dock to Lancaster (enquiries: (05240) 841109)
Car park:	Signposted in Lancaster
Public transport:	British Rail Lancaster

From the bus station in central Lancaster, turn left into Cable Street and then left again into King Street. Continue along this road which eventually becomes Penny Street, goes over a major road junction and then over the canal at Penny Street Bridge.

The last commercial traffic on the Lancaster Canal (a load of coal) was landed at Storey's White Cross Mill, here by Penny Street Bridge in 1947. Curiously, as recently as December 1988, an unexploded bomb was found under the bridge. It was only uncovered when the canal had been drained for routine maintenance work.

The walk to Glasson starts by turning right to walk along the left bank. This area of the canal in Lancaster was once a busy spot and the old Aldcliffe basins and wharves are still vaguely discernible, despite the DIY superstore, on the opposite bank. When the canal was operational, the company had its offices near the basin area. The Waterwitch pub, which we

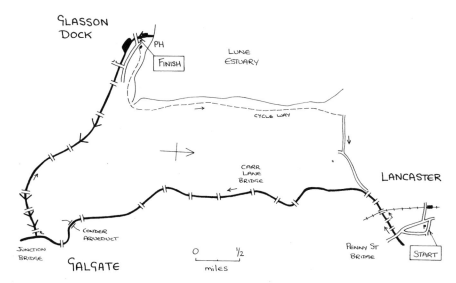

GLASSON DOCK

PH

FINISH

LUNE ESTUARY

CYCLE WAY

CARR LANE BRIDGE

LANCASTER

CONDER AQUEDUCT

JUNCTION BRIDGE

GALGATE

0   ½

miles

PENNY ST BRIDGE

START

The Lancaster Canal

pass shortly on this side of the canal, has been housed in the old stables. The footbridge, however, is of much more recent vintage: January 1987. We walk on to pass a British Waterways yard on the left to reach bridge 98; a fine turnover bridge which allowed barge horses to change banks without having to uncouple from the boat. Of note here are the rope-wear marks on the protecting metals. Our route now continues on the right-hand bank. On the opposite side is another old wharf with a crane still in position and a rather derelict looking building known as the Boat House. At one time packet-boats were refitted here. The boats were pulled out of the water by means of pulleys positioned on the upper floor of the building.

Continue under the railway bridge (No. 97) and on to pass Aldcliffe Road Footbridge. Robert Swain assures us that this was once a ship's gangway. It was put here in May 1954 to replace the old pitch-pine bridge which once occupied this spot. After Haverbreaks Bridge we enter more open country although, for a short distance, a road accompanies the canal to the right. Before too long, however, it veers right and we start along the approaches to the 1½ mile long Deep Cutting. It's a deep, dank, mouldy, cavernous place that in autumn, when I was here, had a peculiarly eerie feel to it. Even the ducks looked a little spooked. In the midst of the chasm, the canal passes under bridge 93: Carr Lane or Broken Back Bridge. It's notable for instead of a conventional stone parapet, the central section of both sides is railed.

After bridge 92 (Burrow Beck Bridge), the sides of the cutting subside a little although the sides of the canal remain heavily wooded and enchanting.

The turnover bridge at the junction between the Glasson arm and the Lancaster main line

The views open out and, for the next mile, we pass through open country-side, rich in herons and passing sparrowhawks. Only gradually do you notice the arrival of civilization in the form of Galgate to the left. After bridge 88 (Ellel Hall Bridge), the canal crosses an aqueduct over the River Conder before swinging left and then right under Galgate Bridge. Here is the Galgate Marina and shortly thereafter a lock-keeper's cottage and Glasson Junction turnover bridge. The line straight on continues towards Preston, we meanwhile go right to reach, almost immediately, the first lock on the Glasson branch.

The 2¹/₂ mile long Glasson branch was authorized by an Act passed on 10 May 1793. The aim was to provide the canal with a sea connection and to improve the fortunes of the Lancaster section of the waterway. Despite this relatively early enabling Act, work wasn't begun until the passage of a further Act on 14 June 1819 which allowed the company to raise the necessary funds. The new branch was surveyed by William Crosley who estimated the cost to be £34,608. Again the work was delayed and the decision to proceed wasn't made until 1823. Part of the reason for this latter delay was the fact that Crosley was considering an alternative line from Hest Bank (north of Lancaster). Hest Bank was already being used as a transhipment point from coastal vessels, even though there was no physical connection between the sea and the canal. Crosley's estimate for the Hest Bank connection was, however, roughly twice that of the Glasson branch. The branch was finally opened in December 1825, and by 1831 the Hest Bank port was closed and the Hest Bank Shipping Company transferred its business to Glasson. The line carried coal destined for North Wales, Ireland and Ulverston and imported slate, timber and grain for the growing town of Preston. The arm is fed from the River Conder. There are six locks altogether and eight bridges (including the turnover bridge at the junction). Although Miller's Canalside Tavern (by lock 6) may arrest your progress for a while, it's an easy 3/4 hour stroll with the massive nuclear power stations on the coastline ahead pulling you ever westward. Eventually we pass the diminuitive Christ Church and reach the Glasson Basin; 36,000 square yd of water, 14 ft deep.

To reach Glasson Dock, bear right along the edge of the basin to the Victoria Inn with the Lune estuary stretching out beyond. If you bear left here you can walk on to the swing bridge and the sea lock with the Glasson Dock beyond. The lock can handle vessels up to 98 ft long and 26 ft wide. The upper gates are doubled so that the lock can also protect the basin from high tides. In 1830, 16,036 tons of cargo passed through the dock, most of it remaining waterborne to continue along the canal. This trade continued to be healthy until 1846 when competition from other ports began to affect trade. There were also problems with the sandbanks in the Lune estuary which limited movement in and out of the dock. The Lune was deepened but the effect was short lived and the problem recurred regularly thereafter. Although cargo traffic has ground to a stop, the records suggest that the lock is five times busier now with pleasure boats than it was at the peak of the canal's commercial activity.

Apart from the Victoria Inn, Glasson Dock has a small post office-cum-corner shop just beyond the swing bridge. There is also a café. The stop for buses back to Lancaster is situated just outside the public conveniences next to the Victoria Inn. However, it is possible to walk back along the converted Glasson branch of the old London & North Western Railway (a distance of 5 miles). The line was opened in 1883 but by 1890 traffic was already declining in the face of competition from Preston Docks. By the 1920s it was losing money badly but it struggled on only to be closed on 7 September 1964. The start of the route can be found just after the bus-stop. Turn left down the side of the public conveniences near the bowling green. At the end, turn right to walk along a clear track which is signposted the Lancashire Coastal Way. This skirts the side of the road with the Lune to the left. The line soon bends north to go over the River Conder on a girder bridge. After passing the old station at Conder Green, there are some fine views over the salt-marshes and mud-flats of the Lune estuary. Continue past Ashton Hall and on to reach a barrier. Turn right and follow the road through Aldcliffe. If you bear left at a junction, you will reach the road that runs parallel to the canal. Rejoin the towpath (on the left-hand bank) and walk back to Penny Street Bridge and central Lancaster.

A Cawood-Hargreaves coal boat train leaves Ferrybridge Flood Lock on the Aire & Calder Navigation at Kellingley

Railway viaducts cross the Bridgewater Canal at Castlefield in central Manchester

The Marple Aqueduct on the Peak Forest Canal

Allbright & Wilson's chemical plant on the Sankey Brook Navigation in Widnes

The Double Arched Bridge at East Marton on the Leeds & Liverpool Canal

The Macclesfield Canal at Marple

Ochre-coloured waters on the Bridgewater Canal at Worsley

Lock 1 on the Huddersfield Narrow Canal in Huddersfield

Further Explorations

All of the extant sections of the Lancaster Canal are open for walking and even the dry northern line can be followed into Kendal. However, one of the major sights of the Lancaster Canal, if not the entire UK canal system, can be seen with a walk from Penny Bridge, Lancaster to Carnforth; a distance of approximately 8½ miles (13½ km) with a return by train.

You can get to Penny Bridge following the instructions from the main walk but on reaching the canal, turn left to walk along the right-hand bank. At the next bridge (Friarage Bridge), the towpath changes to the left-hand bank from where it continues its steady course through the centre of Lancaster. There are five more bridges before the canal bends left to cross two aqueducts in quick succession. The first, the Bulk Aqueduct, which crosses the A683, is a concrete affair that dates from the 1960s, the second is one of the wonders of the canal age: the Lune Aqueduct.

The aqueduct must rate as one of Rennie's finest achievements. Over 600 ft long and 60 ft high, it crosses the river by five huge arches. As with the Dundas Aqueduct on the Kennet & Avon, Rennie would have preferred to have built in brick but was forced to use stone by the canal company.

John Rennie's Lune Aqueduct

Work started in January 1794 with the canal company's own navvies building the foundations for the massive piers. By the summer the work was going on 24 hours a day with as many as 150 men engaged. A year on, in July 1795, the piers were ready and Alexander Stevens & Son of Edinburgh, were appointed as contractors to complete the structure. Although Stevens himself died in January 1796, his son finished the work in the autumn of 1797. The aqueduct had cost £48,320 against Rennie's estimate of £27,500 but all who looked on since have agreed that it was worth every penny.

The canal bends sharply left as it makes a quick tour of the suburbs of Lancaster. When the canal bends back right to head in a more northerly direction, views gradually open up over Morecambe Bay. By the time we reach bridge 118, we are firmly in the centre of Hest Bank. Here, in the early days of the canal and before the opening of the Glasson branch in 1826, was an important transhipment wharf. This was the closest point to the sea, and cargo was moved on to coasters for subsequent carriage to Ireland, North Wales and northern Britain.

The canal meanders around the countryside like an old-fashioned Brindley Canal before arriving at Bolton-le-Sands where the Packet Boat Hotel near the old wharf reminds us that this was once a stopping place for the high-speed boat. The final 1^1/$_2$ miles into Carnforth offers some pleasant countryside and tantalizing glimpses of Morecambe Bay. Carnforth is reached at bridge 128 where a children's playground aids towpath navigation. Walk up to the road and turn left. If you continue over a crossroad (with the A6), you will find the railway station which has regular trains back to Lancaster.

Further Information

The Lancaster Canal Trust helps both the preservation and restoration of the canal that bears its name and can be contacted at:

Lancaster Canal Trust,
16 Galloway Road,
Fleetwood,
Lancashire FY7 7BD.

The society publishes a book *The Complete Guide to the Lancaster Canal* and runs a trip boat, the *Ebb & Flow*, from Holme to Cinderbarrow on Sunday afternoons.

The history of the canal, together with walking details for the entire route, is contained within:

Swain, R., *A Walker's Guide to the Lancaster Canal*. Cicerone Press, 1990.

7
THE LEEDS & LIVERPOOL CANAL
Skipton to Barnoldswick

Introduction

The Leeds & Liverpool is the longest single canal (as worked by one company) in Britain. It was also one of the most successful. Yet it took forty-six years to complete and the two committees, one in Lancashire and the other in Yorkshire, had different views on where the canal went and even what it was for.

The L&L starts just north-east of the Royal Liver Building at a terminus basin and exit to the Mersey at Stanley Dock. From there the canal meanders north to Burscough where the Rufford branch heads towards the River Ribble. The main line now heads east to cross the River Douglas at Parbold. At Wigan the line passes the Leigh branch to Manchester before climbing through twenty-three locks and then turning north along the former Lancaster Canal to Whittle-le-Woods. The L&L now turns north-east through Blackburn, Burnley and Nelson to Foulridge where it passes through a 1,640 yd long tunnel. After Barnoldswick the line meanders around some fine Pennine country to Gargrave before turning south-east to Skipton. The canal then skirts Keighley and goes through Bingley and Shipley where there was formerly a junction with the Bradford Canal. The last stretch passes via Apperley Bridge and Rodley before forming a junction with the Aire & Calder Navigation in the centre of Leeds.

Even without the canal interest, this is a fine country walk through the southernmost reaches of the Yorkshire Dales. Towpathing at its best.

History

The Leeds & Liverpool Canal started life in 1764 as a suggestion to link the Aire & Calder Navigation in Leeds with the River Ribble at Preston. The businessmen of Yorkshire were looking to increase supplies of lime, for a cheaper means of transporting coal and for a route for their goods (especially woollen cloth) to Liverpool and the colonial market. Their counterparts in Lancashire were primarily seeking cheaper coal but were also looking to the markets in the east. Liverpool was expanding rapidly both as a port and as an industrial centre based on its import–export trade. This expansion demanded a good communication system with the hinterland and it demanded coal. The Douglas Navigation, which took the course of the River Douglas from the Wigan coalfield to the sea had been opened in 1742 but still the demand could not be met.

Precisely how the two otherwise disparate groups got together isn't clear but John Stanhope, a prominent Bradford landowner, asked John Longbotham to survey a line between the Aire and the Ribble. It was this that was discussed at a meeting in Bradford on 2 July 1766. Longbotham's proposal, which he completed in August 1767, was for a line from Leeds to Preston where one branch would go north to Poulton and the River Wyre (near Blackpool) and a second south to Liverpool. Following the circulation of a rival scheme in August 1767, Longbotham revised his plan to a more direct line from the Aire & Calder in Leeds to the Mersey in Liverpool. This proposal was presented to a group of Yorkshire businessmen on 7 January 1768 and accepted, subject to review by a more prominent canal engineer such as James Brindley. The meeting, held at the Sun Inn in Bradford, also appointed a Yorkshire committee and decided that a Lancashire committee should be formed.

By August Robert Whitworth (as Brindley's assistant) had checked Longbotham's route and a Lancashire committee had been formed. The two committees met on 19 December 1768 in Burnley. Brindley estimated the cost of the new canal (then called the Yorkshire & Lancashire) at £259,777. The route was to run from Leeds to Keighley, Skipton, Barnoldswick and Barrowford. From there the line ran through Whalley, Walton and Eccleston to cross the River Douglas (without any connection) near Tarleton and thence to Liverpool. The meeting supported the plan and agreed to put a bill to Parliament. However, there were already ructions between the two committees. The Yorkshire group was keen to build the cheapest and quickest line to Liverpool. The Lancashire committee, however, basing its main interest on the canal's ability to deliver cheap coal, preferred a route through the coalfields of south Lancashire, most notably those around Wigan. During the course of 1769 the Lancashire committee had its own survey undertaken by John Eyes and Richard Melling. As some technical faults were found in this, a second was undertaken by P.P. Burdett. His proposal took the Lancashire route from Barrowford via Burnley, Blackburn and Chorley to Wigan. From there it passed along the northern side of the Douglas Valley to Parbold where it rejoined Longbotham's line to Liverpool.

The two committees met and decided that the final route should be decided by Brindley. He reported on 11 October 1769 that the line from Colne to Liverpool was 66 miles and would cost £174,324 whereas Burdett's was 87 miles and would cost £240,881. The finances, plus the fact that the Yorkshire committee was able to out-vote their Lancashire counterparts, meant that the Longbotham line was adopted. Many of the Lancashire subscribers promptly withdrew; observing that the proposed route would not provide the benefits they had sought. Indeed, in a bout of spite, they even declared that they would not allow the new line to connect with the Liverpool Docks (which some of them owned).

Whatever the position of some members of the western committee, by 10 January 1770 a joint meeting resolved to promote Longbotham's plan for a barge canal (able to take boats measuring up to 14 ft 4 in wide) to Parliament. Why the Lancashire committee capitulated isn't evident although there may have been some discussion on a junction with the Douglas Navigation, which would thus have given access to Wigan. The Act received its Royal Assent on 19 May 1770; the main opposition coming from the Douglas who wished to protect its water supply. The Act enabled the company to raise £200,000 in £100 shares and a further £60,000 should it be needed. Longbotham was appointed engineer (Brindley having declined the post) and in November building began at both ends of the line.

Plans to forge the link with the Douglas were forwarded with all haste. Discussions with Alexander Leigh, proprietor of the navigation, were held during 1768–9 and resulted in the L&L buying the line; the majority of the shares changing hands in 1771. The strategy was to complete a line that was already being built by Leigh. This cut, started in 1753, had been designed to bypass some of the more convoluted lengths of the Douglas from Parbold (where the L&L crossed on the Newburgh Aqueduct) towards Wigan. Apart from giving access to the Wigan coalfields, the link with the Douglas would also supply the L&L with much needed water supplies. Leigh Cut was opened in 1774 and was celebrated with the ringing of bells, the playing of bands, the firing of salutes and the consumption of refreshments.

By that time most of the Liverpool section had been built, the section from Skipton to Bingley was opened and there were 31 miles of canal in Lancashire and 23 in Yorkshire. Progress was such that by March 1774 the line from Skipton to Thackley near Shipley was finished. Coal and lime traffic along the L&L and the Bradford Canal now started in earnest. By October the Yorkshire end had been further extended to Gargrave. However, funds were already beginning to run low. Work on the aqueduct at Whalley Nab was stopped and expenditure on the rest of the line curtailed. The stretch into Leeds was completed on 4 June 1777; an event that was celebrated by thirty thousand people. The only other significant work during the 1770s was that along the old Douglas Navigation: a line from the

L&L at Burscough to Rufford (the Lower Douglas Navigation) and an extension of the Leigh Cut from Dean into Wigan (the Upper Douglas Navigation) were completed in 1780 and 1781 respectively.

By the early 1780s, 75 miles of canal had been built (Leeds to Gargrave and Liverpool to Parbold) at a cost of £232,016. In addition, £53,434 had been spent to buy the Douglas Navigation. Although some toll income was forthcoming (£2,025 in 1774 rising to £7,352 in 1778 and £13,062 in 1785), finance was critical and the company was forced to borrow. With the onset of the recession caused by the American War of Independence, all building work was stopped. This period of enforced calm allowed the route through east Lancashire to be reconsidered. There had been a significant expansion of the towns of Blackburn and Burnley, and by the 1790s, when raising funds for canal building was relatively simple, re-routeing the line in Lancashire became expedient. Robert Whitworth was appointed engineer in 1790 and an Act passed in June enabled the company to raise a further £200,000. The Act defined a revised line which went slightly south of the original. By 1793 the line was again altered to one similar to that suggested by Burdett nearly a quarter of a century before. Thus the Upper Douglas Navigation to Wigan was to become the main line which would then pass through Blackburn and Burnley. The new line was longer (an important consideration in view of the newly proposed – and 15 mile shorter – trans-Pennine rival Rochdale Canal) but would add some significant new trading points at not much extra cost.

Although some of the proprietors questioned the wisdom of completing the line at all, the construction of the trans-Pennine section was again under way with some of the biggest engineering projects on the line now being built: Foulridge Tunnel, which opened on 1 May 1796, was 1,640 yd long; the Burnley embankment was a mile long and 40 ft high. Although this work was slow and required a further £100,000 through a new share issue, the line, including the Burnley embankment, was open to Henfield, and thence by turnpike to Accrington and Blackburn, on 23 April 1801.

By 1804 the company had spent £554,569 (not including the purchase of the Douglas) and it still didn't have a complete waterway. Maybe it didn't mind. It was already obvious that the L&L was a success with an annual income of £51,838 enabling a dividend of £8 per share. Some 176,000 tons of coal p.a. were now being shipped into Liverpool and the canal was carrying significant quantities of wool; raw bales being carried inland and spun yarn returned for weaving. The textile industry was developing rapidly all along the line with the canal supplying the ever increasing demand for coal.

The L&L realized that its main business would be at the two ends of its line rather than cross-Pennine but it remained committed to completing the stretch from Henfield to Wigan. Work restarted in May 1805 and the section from Leeds to Blackburn was opened in June 1810. The line from there to Wigan was fraught with complex negotiations but, eventually, it was agreed that the L&L would share the southern line of the Lancaster Canal from Johnson's Hillock near Wheelton to Kirkless (a point near Wigan Top Lock). In return, the Lancaster would receive a water supply for its line from the L&L as well as tolls from the L&L's through traffic.

This final section, and hence the L&L Canal, was fully opened on 19 October 1816. Amid much jubilation the first barge left Leeds on the Saturday, spent its nights at Skipton, Burnley, Blackburn and Wigan, and arrived in Liverpool late Wednesday, again amid great celebration. It had taken forty-six years to build and was (if the shared section of the Lancaster is included) 127 miles long. There were forty-four locks on the Yorkshire side, forty-seven on the Lancashire and more than three hundred bridges

A barge is loaded from a railway wagon on a tippler at old Wigan Pier, *c.* 1891

K.C. Ward/The Boat Museum Archive

spanned the canal. It had cost £877,616 (including buying the Douglas) compared with Brindley's estimate of £259,777. The company was in debt to the tune of £400,000.

Shortly after the completion of the Wigan to Blackburn section, a link to Manchester and the rest of the canal system was made. The Leigh branch, opened in December 1820, runs from Wigan to Leigh where it meets the Bridgewater Canal. One consequence of this was that by March 1822 all the locks between Leigh and Liverpool were lengthened to permit the passage of narrow boats which could now enter the canal from Manchester.

Although overspent, the L&L was, virtually as soon as it was fully open, a success beyond the wildest dreams of the promoters. In 1824 the line earnt £94,423 allowing a dividend of £15 per share. This should be compared with Brindley's estimated annual income from tolls at just £20,000 p.a. Trade was primarily in coal which was supplied from the fields of Yorkshire and east Lancashire (especially those around Wigan) to the industrial centres that were developing all along the line. During the early nineteenth century, about 200,000 tons of coal p.a. were delivered to Liverpool; a figure that rose to over 270,000 tons by the 1830s, more than 500,000 tons by 1840 and more than 1,200,000 tons in 1858. Although lime and limestone were important cargo for the L&L, the traffic in them never reached the significance predicted by the Yorkshire committee. This underestimate was more than made up by the massive, and mostly unexpected, volumes of cargo categorized as 'general merchandise'. This traffic commanded a much higher toll rate (at 1½d. per ton) than either coal (up to 1d.) or limestone (½d.) and was thus a highly profitable business. The term 'general merchandise' covered everything from foodstuffs to night soil and manure, from flax to yarns, from snuff to cast iron, from beer to gunpowder.

They started talking about the possibility of a railway between Liverpool and Manchester in 1822 and, although several bills were defeated in Parliament, the line was opened on 17 September 1830. Meanwhile a less significant line that ran from Bolton to Leigh had already opened for goods traffic in May 1828. There were some thoughts of lowering tolls to compete but in fact it was the railway companies that struggled initially. A minimum toll agreement was made, for example, with the Bolton & Leigh in 1833; not to protect the L&L's income but to bale out the railway. In Yorkshire the rail threat arrived in 1824 with the suggestion for a line from Leeds to Hull. At first this was countered by some major improvements along the Aire & Calder Navigation. But in 1830 the Leeds & Selby Railway Act was passed. The L&S's natural extension, the Liverpool & Leeds, which would have followed the canal through the Wigan coalfield was initially lost in Parliament in 1831 but was passed in 1836 as the Manchester & Leeds Railway.

At first the railways were unable to compete with the canal for its coal and limestone traffic. Part of the reason for this was the fact that much of the industry that used these materials had been built close to the canal and thus the waterway remained the most convenient mode of transport. Gradually, of course, new works would be built near the railways but this transfer of traffic was slow. This meant that by the 1840s, when the number of railways was increasing (the Leeds & Bradford, for example, was opened in 1846), the L&L was still prospering. In 1838 the L&L carried 2,220,468 tons of cargo. In 1840 income totalled £164,908 and dividends from 1841 to 1847 topped £34. In 1847 the company finally paid off its debt.

From the opening of the canal until 1850 the company continued to improve its waterway. One enforced improvement was at Foulridge Tunnel where a partial collapse in 1824 closed the line for eighteen months. Apart from this, some stretches of the line were deepened and several new warehouses built. There were also continuous improvements at the Liverpool terminus. The most important of these was a new, direct link with the Mersey Docks that was engineered by Jesse Hartley at a cost of £42,622. The arm went by four locks to a new dock, Stanley Dock, and was opened in 1848. There was also during this period a programme of reservoir construction. Originally the line was supplied from watercourses but this was soon seen to be inadequate, and by the end of the nineteenth century there were seven reservoirs with a total capacity of 1,174 million gallons.

In 1847, when the L&L started its own carrying fleet, railway competition was beginning to bite into the profitable merchandise traffic in Lancashire (although not yet in Yorkshire). This didn't mean that the railways were thriving. They, too, found that the necessary toll cuts were eating their profit margins. But by 1850 the situation was beginning to change. In 1847 the L&L had been forced to reduce its merchandise tolls to 1d. a mile and this, plus the loss of trade to the railway, meant that the company's income in this sector fell from £58,128 to £15,333 in just two years. Although in 1850 nearly 900,000 tons of coal were still being carried annually, total income was down to just £71,523, less than half that of ten years before. The company was forced to reduce its dividend to £15. This financial pressure was also being felt by the railways, and discussions with a group of companies were held from 1848 to 1850. The result was an agreement (in August 1850) in which the railways leased the merchandise tolls on the canal for £41,000 p.a. until 1871 – later extended to 1874. The carrying fleet was also purchased outright for £13,880. This deal provided the L&L with a guaranteed income for a business it looked like losing. Despite having to pay compensation of £4,335 p.a. to the Lancaster Canal, the company must have been overjoyed with the agreement. Indeed, the L&L prospered thereafter, with dividends returning to £25 by 1856. The merchandise lease certainly had the effect of moving customers onto rail. Whereas canal merchandise traffic totalled 360,000 tons for an average of 30 miles in 1840, by 1871 it was only 282,485 for 12 miles. However, the canal's coal traffic was booming. In 1866, 1,897,000 tons were carried along the line – most on the east Lancashire section. When the merchandise lease came to an end on 4 August 1874, the canal found itself in a strong financial position and ready to compete with a railway system that was becoming increasingly inefficient.

During the course of the railway lease, the L&L made a range of improvements. Steam tugs were working the Liverpool coal trade and various capital works were under way. In 1880 steam powered cargo-carrying fly-boats were introduced, able to tow three or four unpowered boats. The efficiency of this timetabled service meant that the canal was able to attract back much of the merchandise traffic that had been lost. It was said that the canal company provided better warehousing and was actually quicker than the railway between, for example, Burnley and Liverpool. The end of the nineteenth century saw part of the old basin at Liverpool being sold to the Lancashire & Yorkshire Railway. This earnt the L&L £185,341, which it spent renovating the facilities at its western terminus.

Although trade at the end of the century was still good, the passage of the Railway and Canal Traffic Act of 1888 forced the L&L to charge toll rates similar to those of a railway competitor. In general this was about half what it had been charging. With other constraints upon the L&L's activity that were imposed with the passing of the canal's own Act of 1891, profit levels fell dramatically. A dividend of £15 in 1890 was down to just over £4 in 1900 and to nothing in 1901. This was despite the fact that the line was still carrying 1.1 million tons of coal and 600,000 tons of general merchandise annually. The 1891 Act had been introduced to restructure the company and to implement a series of improvements by raising £275,000 in share capital. The plan was to upgrade the canal into one that could handle boats able to carry 67 tons. However, the financial stringency that followed meant that much of this work had to be scaled down considerably. A bad winter in 1895, which closed the canal for two months, and a series of dry summers, didn't help. But trade remained good. In 1906 the L&L carried 2,337,401 tons of cargo to produce an income of £180,000.

The beginning of the end really came in 1917 when the line was brought under government control through the rest of the war and on to 1920. Although the government paid compensation, the company's finances were now in a sorry state and the carrying company was all but broke. Poor wages meant that boat crews were hard to find and continuing losses meant that the activity was closed on 30 April 1921 and the vessels sold. From then to the time of nationalization in 1948, the L&L steadily declined. Various

Barnoldswick Bridge and Greenberfield Lock. The old canal line is visible to the right of the cottage by the bridge, *c.* 1905

Ware/The Boat Museum Archive

parts were sold or closed. The Bradford Canal, for example, which had been jointly owned by the L&L and the Aire & Calder since 1877, was closed in 1922. The situation was partially rescued by the construction of three canalside power stations at Wigan, Whitebirk and Armley, but by the 1950s the canal was declining rapidly and many locks and bridges were in a poor condition. Income in 1956 was £127,500 and the canal lost £132,500. Commercial traffic effectively ended with the great freeze of 1962–3 when traders were unable to move boats for many weeks. The last commercial traffic on the waterway was the delivery of coal from the Plank Lane colliery to Wigan power station in 1973.

The L&L was not viewed enthusiastically by the Board of Survey in 1955 but at least they considered it worthy of retention. The canal never faced the same kind of threat that closed its fellow cross-Pennine routes via Rochdale and Huddersfield. Later, in the 1968 Transport Act, the line was classified as a cruising waterway and, apart from a short section at the Liverpool terminus, is maintained as such today.

The Walk

Start:	Skipton (OS ref: SD 988515)
Finish:	Barnoldswick (OS ref: SD 882474)
Distance:	12¹/₂ miles/20 km
Map:	OS Landranger 103 (Blackburn & Burnley)
Return:	A number of buses run between Barnoldswick & Skipton even on Sunday (enquiries: (0282) 831263)
Car park:	Several well signposted in Skipton or on-street near Rolls Royce Bankfield site, Barnoldswick
Public transport:	British Rail Skipton

The walk starts at the bus station in Skipton. This is a short walk from the centre of town and is well signposted. Cross the small footbridge which leaves the far side of the bus area to go over the canal and then turn right to walk along the left-hand bank.

The canal reached Skipton from Bingley in April 1773 (it didn't open to Leeds until June 1777) when two boatloads of coal were sold to some lucky punters at half the previous price. The occasion was greeted with the ringing of bells, the lighting of bonfires and what the *Leeds Intelligencer* described as 'other demonstrations of joy'. From then on the town became an important canal centre. It was, for example, the headquarters of one of the largest private carrying fleets on the L&L. The canal company itself also had a depot

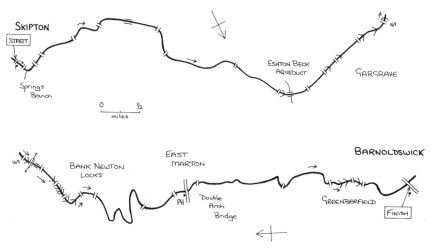

The Leeds and Liverpool Canal

here. Today there are still a number of old canal buildings including a ware-house that has been converted into a pub.

A short way along the towpath we go under Belmont Bridge to where the Springs branch enters the L&L on the opposite bank. This short (770 yd) arm heads along a narrow channel towards Skipton Castle. It was built for the Earl of Thanet, the owner of the castle, to carry limestone from his quarry at Skipton and, later, that at Haw Bank near Embsay. It was probably opened in 1773–4 and was extended in 1797 from the Watermill Bridge through the deep rock cutting. Chutes were constructed at the terminus to drop rock into waiting boats. The Haw Bank quarry, which was some 3/4 miles from the branch, was connected to the line by a horse tramway. When opened, the quarries were being worked by the Mercer Flatts Lime Company but from 1785 the canal company took over the lease which it held through to nationalization. In the 1830s annual production was about 80,000 tons p.a. Most of it was shipped down the canal for use in ironworks or for burning in the many limekilns along the line. The branch gradually declined in importance after Haw Bank was connected to the Midland Railway in 1889. However, an attempt to resurrect the canal trade was made in 1964 when small amounts were shipped out from Haw Bank, which is still being worked. If you have the time, it is well worth a quick stroll along the arm to the terminal basin.

The canal leaves Skipton heading due west, passing the backs of several terraced houses. The line goes over a small aqueduct and then under two swing bridges: Brewery and Gawflat. After passing under the new(ish) A629(T) fly-over bridge, we reach Niffany Swing Bridge where the towpath moves on to the pavement of the road before re-establishing itself through a wooden gate. Already the countryside is becoming more remote, and after another small aqueduct the line goes under the second of the new(ish) flyovers. After passing two more swing bridges (Thorlby and Highgate), we go under Holme Bridge and on to Holme Bridge Lock. Here, for a short distance, the canal acts as the southern boundary of the Yorkshire Dales National Park. In 1882 it was planned to build a reservoir on the northern side here but the plan was dropped following objections from the local landowner Lord Hothfield. The water would have come from Eshton Beck, which the L&L crosses via aqueduct shortly after the lock.

Like many of the bridges along the L&L, Ray Bridge (No. 172) has a white band painted around its arch together with a vertical stripe on the side of the arch to mark the centre of the navigable channel. These markings were painted to help with night navigation. We reach Gargrave at Eshton Road Bridge where we are forced to rise up to and then cross the road. On its westward march, the Yorkshire end of the canal reached Gargrave in March 1774 and there it stayed until October 1790 before the building work recommenced. The construction of the line to here was important as the main water supply for the Yorkshire end fed into the canal from Eshton

Beck. Once the through line was fully operational, the town became an important staging post and it boasted both a warehouse and stabling.

The canal goes through Eshton Road Lock and past the old coal wharf. At Higherland Bridge, the Pennine Way crosses the canal. We, meanwhile, move on to Higherland Lock. One of the more curious things about the locks on the L&L is the variety of ground paddle gear, and Higherland Lock exhibits one of the simplest. Here, just beyond the upper gates, are two wooden structures which look like an extra pair of ill-fitting gates. They're not! These simple wooden barriers are moved sideways to cover or uncover the ground holes.

Continue under Anchor Bridge (cross here for The Anchor Inn) and on to Anchor and Scarland Locks. Stegneck Bridge is followed by Stegneck Lock and the bridge that carries trains from Leeds to Settle. After Priest Holme Aqueduct the towpath changes sides at Priest Holme Changeline Bridge. It is necessary to walk along the road for a short distance before being able to regain access to the towpath via a gate. The canal now makes a straight course, past a lock-keeper's cottage, to the first of the Bank Newton Locks. There are six altogether and the canal twists and turns in order to gain height in as short a distance as possible. After the first lock is Carpenters Yard Bridge and the old canal company yard where maintenance boats were built. The yard acted as the store for the company's legal papers during the Second World War. After the fourth lock is Plantation Lock Bridge. On your way up the flight it's worth noting another piece of canal architecture which, at first, tests the intellect a little. I'm only able to explain it following the advice of Mike Clarke (see Further Information). At the far corner of each lock is an upright metal hook. When the barge was ready to leave the lock, the towrope coming from the horse was passed through a pulley on the boat's towing mast and then forwards on to the hook. The pulley system thus effectively provided the horse with a first gear with which to get the boat moving. After a certain distance a short stick attached to the rope would get trapped in the pulley, the rope would become detached from the hook and the system would then revert to normal towing without any attention from the boatman.

Above the sixth lock the canal reaches Newton Changeline Bridge where the towpath changes sides. Again, we have to walk along the road for a short section before being able to regain access to the towpath. After Newton Bridge the canal enters into a wonderfully convoluted section. For the next half an hour you will approach the TV mast on the hill ahead from virtually every conceivable angle. Although built during the early part of the nineteenth century, the highly circuitous route between here and Barnoldswick is almost a throwback to the age of Brindley. Here we see an unashamed contour canal that follows the line of the country rather than beating a bold straight course over the top of it. Amateur canal engineers can work out whether the line should have been built on the other side of the valley. Some of the bends of the actual line are so acute that the company installed large vertical rollers on the inside corners for the tow lines to run on. None of these are still in position although one of the roller stands remains (examples still exist in Wigan – see Further Explorations).

Eventually the route straightens and heads south-west via Langber Bridge and then Williamson Bridge to reach East Marton. The next bridge on the line is the famous Double Arched Bridge where a second arch has been built half-way down to strengthen the structure. Those more interested in quenching their thirst than the structure of bridges should go underneath and up the side. At the road turn left for the Cross Keys pub.

There is now a quiet 2 mile walk that goes under Old Hall and South Field Bridge before reaching the newly (and splendidly) built Greenberfield Changeline Bridge where the towpath changes sides. Greenberfield is one of those little hot spots of canal interest. The main focus is in the fact that at one time there was a three-lock staircase here. This was replaced by three separate locks in 1820 in order to save water. As you approach Greenberfield Bottom Lock, a slight depression on the right marks the course of the original line. Although the channel disappears after Greenberfield Middle Lock, look right to see the old route going through a garden and on to a redundant canal bridge. Continue past Greenberfield Lock Bridge and up to Greenberfield Top Lock. The old canal bridge is now just to the right and the site of the former staircase is buried under a well-manicured lawn. Both the old route and the new bring the canal up to the summit pound, 487 ft above sea-level. The next lock west is at Barrowford, approximately 6 miles on. Further along there is a lock-keeper's cottage to the right. An information notice informs its readers that lock-keepers have lived here since 1816 and that the first occupant was a retired army captain by the name of Isaac Jones. Just beyond the cottage is another small building dated 17 August 1893. This marks the arrival of the feeder pipe from the Winterburn reservoir which is 9 miles to the north (just south-east of Malham).

It is now just a short stroll into Barnoldswick. After Greenberfield Bridge the canal bends right and then left to pass a redundant bridge (No. 155) and the Rolls Royce Bankfield site to right. The next bridge is Coates Bridge. Go underneath and turn right to reach the road. Turn left and cross the road to reach the bus-stop for transport back to Skipton.

Further Explorations

Virtually all 127 miles of the L&L are open for walking and much of it has been developed with walkers and cyclists in mind. It would make a fine long-distance walk over the course of, say, seven or eight days.

For a single walk of about 12 miles in the Wigan area, park the car at

Burscough, near Burscough Bridge railway station (OS Landranger 108, ref: SD 444124). From the station turn right and walk for about 250 yd to the canal. Turn left to go along the left-hand bank and under Burscough Bridge. Before setting out, it's worth bearing in mind that although cyclists need a permit to ride on BW towpaths, the stretch from Burscough to Wigan was upgraded in 1984 in an attempt to encourage wider use by those with bicycles. You should therefore keep your eyes and ears open as, on summer weekends, cyclists hurtle along the canal and expect towpathers to get out of the way with minimal warning.

The town of Burscough was once an important staging post on the Wigan–Liverpool packet-boat run. The L&L had a yard here where horses could rest and where the company's store of horse provend (i.e. feed) was kept. By the second half of the nineteenth century, Burscough was the centre of the canal's merchandise trade; gaining further importance after the provend depot and vet centre was established here in 1888. Houses, often including stabling, were built for the boatmen alongside the canal from New Lane to Parbold. There was even a mission in the hay loft of the shop at Crabtree Lane. Perhaps most notoriously, Burscough was the point to which manure and night soil were delivered from the cities prior to distribution to local farms. The smell from the accumulated heaps was, perhaps not surprisingly, objected to rather strongly by the local residents. Just before a railway bridge (the Preston to Liverpool line) is Ainscough's Mill with its fine, if dilapidated, canalside awning. The mill received its grain supplies from Liverpool Docks. It also received coal via the canal and the mill owners worked the last horse-drawn boat along the L&L, the *Parbold*, which ended service as recently as 1960. After going under the railway the towpath goes over the roving bridge that marks the entrance of the 7$1/4$ mile long Rufford branch. Opened in October 1781, the line falls by seven (72 ft by 14 ft) locks to a tide lock into the River Douglas at Sollom and then on along the old Douglas Navigation to the Ribble. At the junction are a series of canal cottages, including boatmen's houses on the right, together with a dry-dock. The first two locks along the branch can be seen from the roving bridge.

Along the main line the canal passes through the low-lying, market-gardening farmland and past Glovers Swing Bridge, Ring-o-Bells Bridge, Moss Bridge and Spencer's Swing Bridge. On several occasions the line cuts across minor roads by means of one-arch aqueducts. At Parbold the canal crosses the River Douglas on the Newburgh Aqueduct. This aqueduct was nearly destroyed in June 1838 when a sudden storm caused the river to flood to such an extent that the structure was nearly washed away. As this was the busiest, and hence financially most important, stretch of the L&L, emergency repairs continued 24 hours a day for almost a fortnight. During this time a wooden aqueduct was put into position to allow boat movement.

A little further on is Parbold Bridge. This was formerly called Windmill Bridge because of the old mill which stands on the southern bank. The mill received its grain supplies and exported its flour via the canal.

Beyond Windmill Bridge, look for a blocked arm that leaves the line on the opposite bank. The route between Parbold and Barrowford, as defined in the 1770 Act, was to go through Whalley, Leyland and Eccleston. The towns of Blackburn and Burnley were to be served by branch canals and Wigan by the Douglas Navigation. This blocked arm is all that remains of a length of the original route that was built before the change of course was decided. At one time it was used as a graving dock where the bottoms of boats were burnt clean and then tarred.

We now pass Alder Lane Bridge and Chapel House Bridge to reach Gillibrand Bridge. It is interesting to note the wartime defences that were built along this section of the L&L. Keen-eyed towpathers will already have spotted the pillboxes but at Gillibrand Bridge, among others, there are large concrete anti-tank obstacles that were designed (if such a word can be used) to block the bridges over the canal. After Hand Lane Bridge the canal splits into two channels and the three Appley Locks. The original line (that nearest the towpath) bears just one 12 ft deep lock which almost immediately caused problems. As the locks above Appley (into Wigan) were built with less fall (typically 6–7 ft), there were water shortages. As a consequence, a new channel was built with two locks of more conventional fall and this appears to have improved the situation. At one time both channels were operated with one acting as a sidepond to the other in order to save water. This also had the advantage of speeding traffic flow. Nowadays the original, deeper lock is used. All the locks along this stretch were originally built to take the Yorkshire barges and were 61 ft long by 14 ft 4 in wide. However, when the Leigh branch from Wigan to Manchester was opened in 1821, it was decided to extend all the locks between the branch and Liverpool so that conventional Midland narrow boats could navigate the line. Thus the locks along here are all 72 ft long.

Appley Bridge is marked by an old stone quarry wharf and a series of canal cottages. One of the latter has been converted into the Kettle's On tea shop while, on the other side of the canal is The Railway pub. From here the canal winds through some pleasant open country with the River Douglas winding around the fields to the right. We pass three swing bridges (Finch Mill, Ranicar's and Fisher's) before reaching Dean where there are two extant locks and the remnants of a third in the shadow of the M6. The first lock on this site was the old river lock which ran from the Upper Douglas Navigation down to the River Douglas. This can be seen blocked off to the right (it was closed in the 1880s). This was the original terminus of the Leigh Cut to Wigan which was completed in October 1774. The section from Dean into Wigan was opened in 1781. However, the lock between the river and the new navigation was kept in use so that boats could reach the coal staithes on the opposite side of the river which were served by a number of tramways. The next Dean Lock (the central one) was opened when the Upper Douglas Navigation to Wigan opened in 1781. Later the locks were doubled up to enable two-way passage.

After going under the M6 and the railway bridge, the canal reaches Gathurst where, near Gathurst Bridge, is The Navigation pub. The outskirts of Wigan start at Crooke and soon we bid farewell to the pleasant rural scenery. Here, into the mid-1950s, the John Pit colliery delivered its product via a tramway to the canal edge. It was then tippled directly into waiting barges for delivery to Wigan power station, Ainscough's Mill, Liverpool gasworks, Tate & Lyle's sugar refinery and elsewhere. The staithe was positioned on the Gathurst side of the Crooke Hall Inn. Just on the other side of Crooke Bridge, on the northern bank, was another conduit of coal, this time a branch canal known as the Tunnel Canal. This arm, which was active from 1798 to around 1850, went north into an underground colliery near the Standish and Follient Woods. It was worked by narrow boats similar to those used on the Bridgewater Canal at Worsley.

After Grimshaw's Bridge the canal passes the remnants of the former Crooke Lock (the lock chamber and the gate recesses can still be seen) and under Martland Mill Bridge to reach Hell Meadow Lock. With increasingly dreary surroundings, the line goes under the railway and by Pagefield Lock to continue towards central Wigan. Although the Yorkshire committee was never keen to have the L&L running to Wigan, the coal-hungry, Lancashire committee eventually had its way. The first line from Liverpool, which utilized the Leigh Cut and then the Douglas Navigation for the final stretch, opened in October 1774. The L&L itself arrived in 1781.

The line enters central Wigan by passing under a footbridge, a railway bridge and Seven Stars Bridge. The line then bends sharply left to reach Wigan Pier. The canal basin at Wigan has been developed into a major tourist attraction with many of the restored canalside warehouses and mill buildings open to the public. One part, for example, includes an exhibition entitled 'The Way We Were'. The pier itself, made famous by various sources including George Orwell, was the end of a tramway which brought coal to the canal from local collieries. The pier was built in 1822 and, at its peak, tippled 50,000 tons of coal a year into waiting canal barges. The tippler was dismantled in 1929. The precise site of the pier is marked by the upturned railway lines that hang over the canal. On the opposite bank, where there are now gardens, was also a coal loading wharf. Further along on that side is the first of the canal warehouses. The nearest was built in the 1890s and now houses the exhibition centre. The brick warehouse beyond it, with the covered hoist, is ten years older and now houses a pub/restaurant (The Orwell). This once sported a similar canopy to the exhibition centre

Wigan Pier: the tourist resort

but it was removed during the Second World War. This latter warehouse and the one opposite it on the towpath side were both used to store cotton prior to delivery to the many local mills. The stone warehouse which adjoins the pub and the terminal warehouse (the one that incorporates two entrances for canal barges) are earlier than the others, being built in the 1790s and 1770s respectively. All these buildings were scheduled for demolition in 1973 but, thankfully, British Waterways refused. By 1979 even BW thought that they should be knocked down but by then the terminal warehouse had been listed and thus it was the local authority's turn to do the refusing. In 1982 the County Planning Officer recognized the potential of the site, and by 1984 the restoration progress was complete.

Continue over Pottery Changeline Bridge and turn left to descend to the left-hand bank. Underneath the bridge are restored examples of the rollers that protect the bridge arches from towline wear. On the other side of the bridge there are a group of canal cottages followed by Trencherfield Mill on the left. The building presently on this site was peculiarly old-fashioned in being built next to the canal rather than the railway. A little further on, the towpath crosses the mill's own canal arm and dock to which coal and cotton were delivered. On the opposite bank is a hire boatyard that was formerly the site of James Mayor & Co., boat-builders. Within a short distance we reach Wigan Bottom Lock. The twenty-three Wigan Locks raise the canal just over 214 ft in approximately 2$1/2$ miles. The second lock of the flight is reached after crossing the busy (and tricky to cross) Chapel Lane at Henhurst Bridge. This bridge was important because the towpath for boats heading for Manchester changed to the right-hand bank whereas those going to Leeds stayed on the left. The cottages on the towpath side of the lock formerly housed the lock-keeper and toll collector. The toll office was later transferred into the smaller red-brick building to the right.

The line crosses a small aqueduct over the River Douglas and goes on to a small bridge that was once the canal entrance to the Wigan Electric Light and Power Company. The opening is now blocked but a small culvert a little further on is open and delivers water into the pound from the River Douglas. From here the main line of the canal goes straight ahead on its way to Leeds, some 92 miles to the east. The right turn, meanwhile, heads towards Manchester, 23 miles to the south-east. This is the Leigh branch which runs for 7$1/4$ miles to the town of Leigh where it forms a junction with the Bridgewater Canal and hence provides a through route to central Manchester and the rest of the canal system. The line was originally proposed in 1803 but it took some time to reach agreement with the proprietors of the Bridgewater and to fight off the opposition of the Rochdale and the Manchester, Bolton & Bury Canals. It wasn't until June 1819 that the line received its Royal Assent. It was opened in December 1820 at a cost of £61,419.

To complete the walk, return to Pottery Changeline Bridge. Go underneath and bear right and then left to cross a new bridge in front of the terminal warehouse. Turn left here to visit the Wigan Pier exhibitions. To reach Wigan Wallgate station, go straight on and cross the road. Turn right and walk towards the town centre. Go under a railway bridge and continue on to pass the North Western train station on your right. A hundred yards further on, the Wallgate station is on the left. For enquiries on trains back to Burscough Bridge ring: (0942) 42231.

One of the great short strolls on the canal system, let alone the L&L, is at Bingley, a few miles north-west of Bradford on the A650 Keighley road (OS Landranger 104, ref: SE 110392). You can park near Bingley station (train enquiries: (0532) 448133) in a huge car park by the canal. Go through the gate and turn left to walk along the left bank. Almost immediately, you pass the waterbus stop (for enquiries about trips phone: (0274) 595974) and go under Park Road Bridge. The canal hereabouts is being shifted right at a cost of £4.5 million to accommodate some road-works. Luckily it shouldn't alter the character of the spot too much and the canal will still sit in the shadow of the massive Bowling Green Mill that is now home to Damart thermals.

Continue around the canal bend to the first lock rise: the Bingley Three Rise. This is a staircase of locks in which the top gates of one lock act as the bottom gates of the next. Such structures were used to overcome sharp height changes. The problem is that a boat has to pass up all three locks

Bingley Five Rise

before another can come down. Above the flight, the canal bends gradually left through a pleasantly wooded stretch and on to the main course for this trip: the Bingley Five Rise.

This magnificent set of locks is based on the same principle as the three rise. However, the extra two locks plus an altogether more grandiose architecture make this a real tourist spot. The locks were designed by John Longbotham and were completed in 1770. Even then the five rise was seen as something extraordinary and it had its own opening ceremony which included bands playing, guns firing and local church bells ringing. Each lock measures 62 ft by 14 ft 4 in and holds 90,000 gallons of water. Altogether they take the canal up 60 ft. I'm told that this can be done in thirty minutes although when I was here, a stream of boats seemed to arrive at the bottom, took one look at the climb and returned back the way they came.

You can walk up the flight either via the path to the left or on the opposite bank. At the top there is a swing bridge and some canal buildings. If you're the lucky sort, you may also find the ice-cream stand open for refreshment prior to your stroll back to the car.

Further Information

There is no Leeds & Liverpool Canal society as such but the Inland Waterways Association has local branches that cover the waterway. For further information contact the London office (see Appendix B).

For information on the Leeds & Liverpool Canal look no further than:

Clarke, Mike, *The Leeds & Liverpool Canal.* Carnegie Press, 1990.

8
THE MACCLESFIELD CANAL
Macclesfield and Bollington

Introduction

Wedged between the busy Trent & Mersey and the scenic Peak Forest, the Macclesfield Canal is almost overlooked as it skirts the Peak District National Park on its route from the Potteries to Marple. It doesn't deserve to be.

At its southern end, the Macclesfield leaves the Trent & Mersey Canal just north of the Harecastle Tunnels at Hardings Wood Junction, Kidsgrove. From there it crosses the T&M at Pool Lock Aqueduct and heads north through open country to Congleton. The canal fits its twelve functional locks into a little under a mile at Bosley before continuing along a meandering course to reach the eastern edge of Macclesfield. From there, the line passes through Bollington and High Lane before reaching the Peak Forest Canal at Marple Junction.

Although there is a short section along the busy streets of Macclesfield, this circular walk has bags of interest including a return stroll along the Middlewood Way.

History

During the latter half of the eighteenth century there had been several attempts to raise interest in a waterway between the Peak Forest Canal at Marple and the Trent & Mersey at Hall Green near Kidsgrove. A canal from Macclesfield to Congleton and Northwich had been proposed in 1765 and a correspondent to the *Derby Mercury* suggested a Caldon Canal–Leek–Macclesfield line in December 1793. In 1795 a group of promoters planned a canal from the Poynton collieries to Stockport. This plan

A LNER trip boat at Bollington in the 1930s

R.W. Lansdell/The Boat Museum Archive

was later extended south through Macclesfield to the Trent & Mersey near Kidsgrove and to the Caldon at Leek. Yet another group of enthusiasts sponsored Benjamin Outram to carry out a survey for a line from the Peak Forest to the Caldon at Endon via Rudyard with a branch canal or railway from Poynton and Norbury to Stockport. This scheme was reported to a meeting on 11 March 1796 at Macclesfield. The cost was estimated at £90,000 with a revenue of £10,175 p.a. At a follow-up meeting in April it was agreed to proceed. However, following some concern over the likely profitability of the new route, and with opposition from the Trent & Mersey, which was promoting its own line from the Caldon to Leek, the plan was dropped. Other schemes were proposed by the Peak Forest Canal Company. In 1799 it considered building a line from Marple to Poynton and Norbury collieries, and in 1805–6 it evaluated the potential for a line via Macclesfield to the Trent & Mersey near Kidsgrove.

Despite all these valiant attempts, it wasn't until 6 October 1824 that the form of what is now the Macclesfield Canal was first proposed. A meeting in the town was held to consider the issue and, almost immediately, some £60,000 was subscribed to the project. It must be said that not all those present were keen on the idea and one far-sighted individual, a Mr Wakefield, was audacious enough to have suggested that a railway might be better. The committee promised to assess both ideas but the mood of the meeting held sway. In November a group of Macclesfield promoters visited the Peak Forest committee. The two parties got on well and agreed that the prospects for the new line would be highly beneficial to both concerns. With the Peak Forest's support, the committee asked Thomas Telford to carry out a survey. He produced two reports and 'most unequivocally' declared in favour of a canal which was to be highly beneficial for the silk and cotton mills and the many other manufacturers in and around the towns of Macclesfield and Congleton. He estimated the cost of construction as £295,000.

The Macclesfield Canal Act was passed in April 1826. Among the shareholders were many of the Peak Forest's promoters, including Samuel Oldknow (see Chapter 9). Even Thomas Telford subscribed £1,000. Despite carrying out the original survey and evaluating the various contractors who had tendered for the work, Telford did not become involved with the construction work. Instead William Crosley, formerly one of the resident engineers on the Lancaster Canal, was appointed as chief engineer. By all accounts the construction work went smoothly and quickly. At the southern end the line ended at Hall Green about a mile from the junction at Hardings Wood, Kidsgrove. That final mile was built by the Trent & Mersey who felt that they needed to exert some kind of control over the traffic travelling north along the new route. As the new line was marginally higher than the Trent & Mersey level, the Macclesfield company built a stop lock at the junction between the two to prevent water loss into the Trent & Mersey.

The new canal opened on 9 November 1831 at a cost of about £320,000 raised in 3,000 £100 shares and a small amount of borrowing. The line is 26^{1}/$_{8}$ miles long from Marple, where it joins the Peak Forest at the top of the Marple flight, to the junction with the Hall Green branch on the summit level of the Trent & Mersey. The only functional locks are the twelve at Bosley which carry the canal up 120 ft to the 518 ft summit level. The line is fed by reservoirs at Bosley and Sutton. The new canal provided a waterway route to Manchester that was 10 miles shorter than that by way of the Trent & Mersey to Preston Brook and then the Bridgewater into Manchester, but with twenty more locks. The opening was celebrated by two processions of boats, twenty-five from the north and fifty-two from the south. The leading boats contained various dignitaries, while following boats were loaded with bands and artillerymen or simply with onlookers. Merchant vessels came shortly thereafter loaded with a wide variety of cargo such as coal, grain, salt, iron, timber, lime, coke, cotton bales and groceries.

Almost from the off, the Macclesfield had to compete with rival routes: the Trent & Mersey for goods going between Manchester and Staffordshire, and the new Cromford & High Peak Railway, which had also opened in 1831. This latter line joined the Peak Forest Canal with the Cromford Canal

A snake, or roving, bridge on the Macclesfield Canal. The design allows the horse to change towpaths without unhitching. Probably 1950s

R.W. Lansdell/The Boat Museum Archive

and was thus a fast route for goods being shipped between Manchester from the Nottingham–Leicester–Buxton area and on towards Chesterfield and Sheffield. The Cromford & High Peak had been authorized in May 1825 and was an important source of trade for the Peak Forest and a potential threat to both the Trent & Mersey and the Macclesfield. In 1837 the new canal faced additional railway competition with the opening of the Grand Junction Railway. The company responded in the only way open to it. It reduced the rates. The company also successfully convinced the Peak Forest to reduce its rates in an attempt to kick-start the business. By July 1833 further reductions were needed. The Trent & Mersey had flexed its muscles and reduced its own tolls in an attempt to keep its Manchester via Preston Brook trade. The vigour of the Trent & Mersey's attack can be seen by the fact that toll reductions were not applied to the Hall Green branch. With these reductions, limestone was being carried for $1/4$d. per ton per mile, lime for $1/2$d., coal for $3/4$d., and merchandise for 1d.

Some trade must have been forthcoming for in 1833–4 the company paid a dividend of 1 per cent. This figure was increased to 2¹/₂ per cent in 1836 and was maintained until 1839. From 1837, however, competition from the Grand Junction Railway was being felt and the Macclesfield's shareholders received the last of their pay-days in 1840–1 with just 1¹/₂ per cent. Any income after that was used to reduce the company's debt. The opening of the GJR stimulated a meeting of the canal companies and carriers on the Manchester–London route to consider the use of steam power and to appraise the situation regarding the Manchester & Birmingham Junction Canal. This 16 mile long canal would have run from the Bridgewater at Altrincham to the Ellesmere & Chester at Middlewich and promised a shorter line from Manchester to the Potteries and Birmingham with less lockage and tunnels. The Manchester & Birmingham Junction was surveyed by W.A. Provis with a proposed capital of £500,000. The Macclesfield, Peak Forest, Trent & Mersey and other companies fought the new line vigorously and successfully with the plan failing to reach Parliament.

There was further concerted action at the beginning of 1839 when the Peak Forest suggested that unless toll reductions were made the railway would take virtually all of the London–Manchester traffic. In particular, accusing fingers were pointed at the Coventry and Oxford companies who were proving obstinate to the idea of lowering tolls. The rates at the time were: 1d. per ton per mile on the Trent & Mersey and Macclesfield, 1¹/₄d. on the Peak Forest, 1¹/₂d. on the Grand Junction, Coventry and Birmingham, and 2d. on the Ashton and Oxford. This meant a total of 28s. 5d. on the London-Manchester line via the Macclesfield Canal. The report convinced the southern companies and later in the year the tolls on the route were down to 21s. 6³/₄d. A further meeting in March 1839 heard that Pickford's had experienced a sudden drop in trade along the three associated canals (the Macclesfield, Ashton and Peak Forest) with the railway companies taking a significant proportion of the light goods traffic. There was also an increase in competition for the Staffordshire iron trade from a newly introduced coaster service importing iron from Scotland. It must be said that the Macclesfield was less energetic in its attempts to fight off railway competition than its neighbours at the Peak Forest. The company had started operating steam boats and, from 1842 (until at least 1846), was operating a fast passenger craft. But it did little else. It was almost as if it was resigned to the inevitable. Its strategy was to cut staff and reduce wages. This allowed it to decrease tolls to the point where much of the merchandise was passing at ³/₄d. or ¹/₂d. per ton per mile. The consequent reduction in income meant that no dividends were paid after 1840.

In July 1845 the North Staffordshire Railway was promoted and this stirred the Macclesfield into some kind of response. The company threatened to build a railway between the Manchester & Birmingham Railway at

Macclesfield, and the lines of the proposed railways at Kidsgrove. Whether or not the plan was of serious intent, the result was that the NSR, who by that time had already agreed to buy the Trent & Mersey Canal Company, offered the Macclesfield shareholders 1,000 shares in return for abandoning their scheme and helping the railway get its Act. The Macclesfield committee supported the scheme but not necessarily the terms. It recommended that its shareholders should agree to lease the Macclesfield to the NSR only if the railway company would offer £2 per share p.a. In October the NSR made an alternative proposal in which it was suggested that the Macclesfield company should subscribe £40,000 to its company and appoint a director, and should give the railway an option to buy the waterway within five years at 50s. a share plus payment for debt. The Macclesfield's shareholders rejected these terms but not the idea. The committee was asked to seek an alternative agreement with any other railway company, or even to seek powers to make a line of its own.

In December 1845 the committee was able to report that the Sheffield, Ashton-under-Lyne & Manchester Railway was prepared to buy the Macclesfield at a perpetual yearly rent of £6,605, equivalent to 50s. a share on 2,642 shares. The deal was to include a payment of £60,000 to cover any outstanding debt. The shareholders agreed at a time when the Trent & Mersey was fighting hard for the Manchester traffic by reducing tolls; a fact which may well have prejudiced the minds of the shareholders. With the enabling Act passed, the Macclesfield, together with its neighbour the Peak Forest, became the property of the Sheffield, Ashton-under-Lyne & Manchester Railway, though the canal company continued as a separate entity, collecting rents, until 1883. The last meeting of the canal company was held on 15 July 1847.

About the first thing the Sheffield, Ashton-under-Lyne & Manchester did with its new possessions was to obtain an Act which allowed it to sell water from either line. Shortly thereafter, the company was approached by the manager of the Navigation Department of the North Staffordshire with a view to the NSR taking over the waterways. However, it later transpired that the approach was made without authority and negotiations were not started. At the time, the Macclesfield was returning annual toll receipts of just over £9,000. In 1848 the Sheffield, Ashton-under-Lyne & Manchester started its own carrying business along the Ashton, the Peak Forest and the Macclesfield. The trade was linked with its own goods yard at Guide Bridge near Ashton-under-Lyne. In 1854, 6,894 tons of the trade along the Macclesfield were carried by the new venture, out of a grand total of 214,445. The traffic was primarily in raw cotton. The company operated the carrying service until 1894 by which time back-carriage was becoming hard to find and the business was closed.

By 1905 traffic had diminished considerably. The prime business along the Macclesfield by this time was still in coal but many of the local collieries were closing. Other cargo included raw cotton, grain (carried from Manchester and other docks) and stone. The decline continued through the two wars and the Stoke-Marple coal trade finally ended in 1954. By then the canal had been nationalized for six years although without great prospect. But the line was not to suffer the almost terminal decline of its Peak Forest and Ashton neighbours. Although the Macclesfield was listed in the Report of the Board of Survey in 1955 as having insufficient commercial prospects to justify its retention, the Transport Act of 1968 listed it as a cruising waterway. On this basis it exists under the guardianship of British Waterways and is a justifiably popular route for holiday cruisers.

The Walk

Start and finish:	Macclesfield railway station (OS ref: SJ 919736)
Distance:	7¹/₂ miles/12 km
Map:	OS Landranger 118 (Stoke-on-Trent & Macclesfield)
Car park:	Several signposted in Macclesfield
Public transport:	British Rail Macclesfield

The walk starts at Macclesfield railway station which is east of the town centre not far from the Buxton Road (A537) and across the street from the bus station. From the railway station turn right and then right again to go under the railway. Our way now bears right to take the road to Buxton. Pass The Bull, then Victoria Park and carry straight on at the next roundabout. Just before the Puss In Boots, the road crosses the canal. On the right is the canalside Hovis Mill. We, however, cross the canal and turn left to take the steps which go down to the towpath.

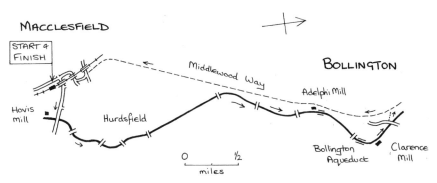

The Macclesfield Canal

The walk starts along the right-hand bank and follows the canal as it bends right past Peak Forest boats and goes under a bridge into open country. In just half a mile, the bustle of Macclesfield gets left behind and all we are left with are the sounds of the birds. The canal now bends back left to go under a skew bridge (No. 35) which, like many along the way, was built of stone which has a pink tinge to it. The Cheshire Ring Canal Walk book (see below) tells us that this highly individual stone comes from the millstone grit quarries at Teg's Nose, a country park about 2 miles east of Macclesfield.

From here the canal goes through Hurdsfield and although we pass close to the houses, the line still has a quiet relaxing air. We pass under an expanded road bridge (No. 34) and on to the first milestone which informs us that Marple is 10 miles off. These stones were removed during the Second World War in case the enemy invaded and used them to find their way about; a move, which with the great aid of hindsight, seems a little ludicrous. Luckily these impressive stones were restored to their former positions by the Macclesfield Canal Society; no mean feat as apparently each weighs about half a ton.

The canal goes under the next bridge (No. 33) and then expands to form a winding hole. There is now a long straight section of canal which has three distinct 'narrows' marking the sites of former swing bridges. Interestingly only two of these are allowed for in the bridge numbers. The site over the fence is a chemical works which, perhaps fortunately, is obscured from our view. The next bridge (No. 30), an accommodation bridge, has a plaque on it which commemorates its reopening by the local MP on 3 August 1991 following reconstruction by the Macclesfield Canal Society. The rope grooves on the sides of the bridge suggest a busy past. There are stop plank grooves underneath the bridge and a rack of planks on the far side.

Shortly we pass another milestone (Marple 9 miles; Hall Green 17¼) and walk on to a fine turnover bridge: Clarks Change Bridge. The design of these wonderfully elegant bridges was immensely practical as they enable the towpath to change sides without the boatman needing to unhitch the horse. Again there is a stop plank rack on the far side; seemingly being embraced by the arms of the turnover bridge. We cross the canal here to continue the walk along the left-hand bank. The path now goes on past Kerridge dry-dock (to the right). This was formerly the dock for a gritstone quarry up on Kerridge Hill beyond. The two were connected by means of a tramway. After curving left to go under bridge 28, the outskirts of Bollington can be seen away to the right and we walk on to Adelphi Mill with the Anglo Welsh boatyard opposite. Adelphi Mill was built in the 1850s for George Swindells, a local cotton manufacturer. He had it built here to take advantage of the canal transport. However, within twenty years, the Macclesfield, Bollington & Marple Railway was opened and the canal was superceded. The mill produced cotton and silk and, after the Second

World War, rayon and nylon for Courtaulds. The mill was closed in the 1970s and has since been converted into smaller industrial units and offices. Near the end of Adelphi Mill is the Macclesfield & Vale Royal Groundwork Trust Discovery Centre and shop. This is open from Tuesday to Sunday in the afternoons. Admission is free. There is also a cycle hire shop here.

At the end of the bridge is the Barge Inn. Central Bollington, which has numerous hostelries as well as a reasonable range of shops, can be reached by descending the steps just after the mill and turning right to go under the aqueduct. For those uninterested in such temptations, continue over this small aqueduct, on through the pleasant Bollington suburbs and under the next bridge (No. 27). The canal crosses the Dean Valley by means of a 60 ft high embankment and a short stone aqueduct: the Bollington or Dean Aqueduct. From the embankment there are fine views of Bollington to the right and of the playing fields and the Bollington railway viaduct to the left.

On the other side of the valley is Clarence Mill. This former cotton mill was built in the 1820s (i.e. at a similar time to the canal) again for the Swindells family. It is firmly canal oriented and has a fine unloading bay where the raw cotton and coal were delivered. In the 1820s the first section

Clarence Mill at Bollington

with the tower was built. It was later extended to the left in the 1850s. The section with the chimney was built in the 1890s and 1900s. The mill produced fine cotton for high quality clothing and table linen. It was closed in the 1960s and is now divided into offices and small industrial units. A little further on a small railway track crosses the towpath. This was used to carry skips loaded with boiler ash from the mill to a dump over the bank.

After going under a fine skew bridge, turn left to go up to the road. Turn right. After 100 yd, turn right along the drive of Lodge Farm. On reaching a fence on the left, cross a stile and then descend the bank on to the tarmacked Middlewood Way. This was formerly the line of the Macclesfield, Bollington & Marple Railway that has now been converted into a path and cycleway. The line was opened on 2 August 1869 and closed on 5 January 1970. It was reopened for walkers and cyclists in 1985. A full description of the Middlewood Way appears in *Railway Walks: LMS* by Jeff Vinter (Alan Sutton, 1990).

Turn left to walk over the Bollington viaduct. It should now be possible to walk on along the Middlewood Way all the way back to central Macclesfield from where local signposts will point you to the station. However, when I was here the route was blocked at Clarke Lane Bridge. If this is still the case (notices will indicate if it is), continue along the course of the line until it reaches a road. Here turn left to walk up to the aqueduct near the Adelphi Mill. If you ascend the steps, you can return to the towpath. Turn right to return to Macclesfield via the canal.

Further Explorations

The whole of the Macclesfield Canal is open for walking and all of it is worth a look. At 27½ miles, very fit towpathers could walk the entire length from Marple to Kidsgrove on one long summer's day. Mere mortals could consider making a weekend of it; spending the Saturday night in Macclesfield itself (for accommodation enquiries ring the tourist information office: (0625) 618228). If you started at midday in Marple, afternoon tea could be had in Bollington before reaching Macclesfield by early evening. A late start on Sunday could permit afternoon tea at the National Trust's Little Moreton Hall, just south of Congleton (about a mile from the canal and well signposted) before walking on to Kidsgrove. Both ends are served by British Rail (enquiries for Marple ring: (061) 228 7811; for Kidsgrove ring: (0782) 411411).

For a simpler afternoon's stroll of approximately 7 miles, start at Kidsgrove railway station (OS Landranger 118, ref: SJ 837544) where there is a car park (fee payable). Almost directly opposite the station itself, a series of steps descends to the Trent & Mersey Canal where the iron-enriched waters shine a brilliant yellow. For those who are not familiar with the T&M at Kidsgrove, you might wish to start the walk by turning right to go along the right-hand bank. Within a short distance the canal reaches the Harecastle Tunnels that take the line south to Stoke-on-Trent and beyond. There are two tunnels here. James Brindley's was the first and is to the right. It is 2,880 yd long and was opened in 1777 having taken eleven years to complete. There were constant problems with a poorly built tunnel through a series of mine workings which led to numerous collapses. As a consequence a 'new' tunnel was built by Thomas Telford. This is the one that is open today. It is 2,926 yd long and was first opened in 1827 having taken just three years to build. It is not without its problems and was extensively renovated during the 1970s. For more information on the T&M, the tunnels and walks along the canal, readers should seek out *Canal Walks: Midlands*.

Return to the steps from Kidsgrove station and walk on along the left-hand bank of the canal. The towpath goes under a road bridge (the entrance to the station) and then the railway itself before reaching a handsome roving bridge at Hardings Wood Junction: the start of the Macclesfield Canal. Cross the bridge and turn left to walk along the right-hand bank. The route creeps around the back of some houses, under another bridge and on to Pool Lock Aqueduct that takes the Macclesfield over the Trent & Mersey in a kind of canal flyover. This is made possible by the fact that the T&M has descended by two locks since Hardings Wood Junction whereas the Macclesfield has stayed at the same level.

Cross the canal at the bridge just before the aqueduct to continue along the left-hand bank. Within a short distance the line goes over a second aqueduct, Red Bull Aqueduct, which spans the busy A50. Already the canal is into the open country that makes this stretch of the Macclesfield so attractive. The canal goes under two bridges to reach the first lock: Hall Green Lock. It is interesting to note that, contrary to expectations, this was the official start of the Macclesfield Canal. The stretch we have walked along so far actually belonged to the T&M who built it in order to have some control over this new short cut to Manchester. The lock, which has a rise/fall of just 12 inches, was built by the Macclesfield company as a stop lock to limit the flow of water into the ever water-hungry T&M. The T&M, in some kind of petty retaliation, then added an extra lock of their own in order to be able to charge a toll for those entering their line. The T&M lock-gates have been removed but the chamber, together with the recesses for the gates, can still be seen on the Kidsgrove side of the present lock.

The walk now passes under a footbridge and then on under six bridges. After passing a milestone (Marple 25 miles), the canal appears to pass

Hardings Wood Junction
where the Macclesfield
Canal joins the Trent &
Mersey

through the grounds of Ramsdell Hall. Curiously the owners of the hall welcomed the building of the commercial waterway through the grounds of
their estate and they even had their own wharf built. For those who wish to
visit the National Trust's Little Moreton Hall, go up to the next bridge (No.
86) and turn left to walk along the lane for about a mile.

From here the canal continues under five bridges and then over Watery
Lane Aqueduct. Three bridges further on and the canal reaches the outskirts of Congleton. Bridge 77 is a splendidly graceful turnover bridge which
takes the towpath to the right-hand bank. Our way passes the warehouse on
Congleton Wharf, the canalside Moss Inn, and then goes over Congleton
Aqueduct. This is not the first aqueduct on this site. The original had to be
pulled down and the present one was built by Thomas Telford. It is a typical Telford design being constructed of an iron trough. Those who are

familiar with the Wootten Wawen Aqueduct on the Stratford and the Nantwich Aqueduct on the Shroppie will recognize the style.

The towpath changes back to the left-hand bank at the next turnover bridge and then enters a deep chasm made by the railway and road bridges and Oakes Millers factory on the right of the canal. Go under the road bridges and turn left to go up some steps to Congleton station where trains will take you back to Kidsgrove.

For a glimpse of the northern terminus of the Macclesfield Canal and the junction with the Peak Forest Canal at Marple see Chapter 9.

Further Information

The address for those interested in joining the Macclesfield Canal Society is:

Macclesfield Canal Society,
'Hawkesbury',
72 Blakelow Road,
Macclesfield,
Cheshire SK11 7ED.

For more details of the history of the waterway:

Hadfield, C., *The Canals of the West Midlands*. David & Charles, 1985 (3rd Edition).

9
THE PEAK FOREST CANAL
Newtown to Whaley Bridge

Introduction

It's a wonderful little canal the Peak Forest and a strangely well-kept secret. It doesn't have the historical significance of the Bridgewater or the sheer effrontery of the cross-Pennine lines like the Rochdale or the Huddersfield Narrow. It was never as busy as the Aire & Calder nor is it ultimately as scenic as the Leeds & Liverpool. Yet it can compete on most of these things and many will argue that it wins hands down. And to think that it very nearly disappeared forever!

The 14^3/$_4$ mile long Peak Forest Canal starts at a junction with the Ashton Canal and the Huddersfield Narrow Canal at the Portland Basin in Ashton-under-Lyne. From here the line goes south through Dukinfield to Hyde. After passing through the Woodley Tunnel the canal continues via Romiley and the Hyde Bank Tunnel to go on over the famous Marple Aqueduct. Here the canal passes through the town of Marple itself, ascending the hill by sixteen locks to a junction with the Macclesfield Canal. The 'upper' level of the PFC now enters rural Cheshire where it runs south-east via New Mills to another junction near Buxworth. Here one arm continues to a terminus at Whaley Bridge, where the Cromford & High Peak Railway formerly offered a route to the Cromford Canal and all points south and east. A second arm goes east to Bugsworth Basin, once the busy terminus for a series of tramroads which delivered limestone from the quarries of the northern Peak District.

You can walk the whole thing or take just a couple of short strolls along the highly accessible towpath. A fine walk on any occasion and the stretch through Marple is as good as you'll find anywhere.

History

The Ashton Canal, a line from Piccadilly in Manchester to Ashton-under-Lyne, was enabled by an Act passed in June 1792. The main purpose of the new canal was as a conduit for the many collieries around Ashton and Oldham but the line was also seen as being a possible first step in a new cross-Pennine route (later to be completed via the Huddersfield Narrow Canal – see Chapter 5). It was only later that the Ashton's shareholders began planning a branch to continue their line on through Marple to the limestone quarries of the northern Peak District.

At a meeting on 8 May 1793 the Ashton promoters agreed to introduce a bill for what would be the Peak Forest Canal. However, when it came to it, it wasn't the Ashton company that made the necessary moves. Instead a wholly independent group held a meeting in July 1793 to review the plans for a scheme to build a line from what is now Portland Basin, Ashton-under-Lyne, through Hyde and Marple to Chapel Milton. The prime purposes for the new canal were firstly to access limestone for burning to lime and secondly to serve the mines and industry between Hyde and Dukinfield. As part of this plan a tramroad was to run from the canal to the limestone quarries at Doveholes, about 4 miles north of Buxton. One of the key movers of the scheme was the cotton baron and chum of Richard Arkwright, Samuel Oldknow. Oldknow had extensive interests along the route and had plans to build limekilns at Marple which would take advantage of the new waterway for supplies of both limestone and coal.

The Peak Forest's Act was passed, with the support of the Ashton company, on 28 March 1794. The Act enabled the company to raise capital of £90,000 and a further £60,000 if necessary. The narrow boat canal was to run for 14³/4 miles from Ashton to Bugsworth (near Whaley Bridge) through three short tunnels and over a substantial aqueduct (at Marple). The line included sixteen locks at Marple rising 209 ft to a summit pound that was 518 ft above sea level. From Bugsworth, the Act enabled the construction of a tramroad to Chapel Milton and a ¹/2 mile long branch to Whaley Bridge. Benjamin Outram was appointed as engineer with Thomas Brown his resident assistant.

Work began at the Ashton Junction at Dukinfield and on the Marple to Bugsworth length. Curiously, although Outram had been appointed engineer, the canal committee spent some years flirting with an American engineer called Robert Fulton. Fulton, together with Charles McNiven, had been contracted to cut part of the line. Although Outram was unhappy with the contractor's work rate, the committee was impressed by Fulton and began preferring his advice to that of its appointed engineer. For a time, for example, it considered Fulton's proposal for an iron-arched aqueduct at

Marple rather than Outram's masonry design. The committee then had Outram following up Fulton's suggestions for converting the canal into one suitable for tub-boats and for the replacement of the planned Marple locks with an inclined plane. The company even paid for the printing of a book by Fulton which expanded on his ideas: *A Treatise on the Improvement of Canal Navigation* (published in 1796). Curiously, Fulton's influence disappeared virtually as quickly as it had arisen. The canal was built as a narrow boat line, the Marple Aqueduct was constructed using masonry and any thoughts of an inclined plane at Marple were quietly forgotten.

By July 1796 work was proceeding apace but already funds were running low and the company found itself with a £4,000 overdraft that it was unable to pay off. Members of the committee were forced to guarantee the monies owing and to advance a further £4,000; a sum that was needed to complete the summit level and the tramroad. Both were opened on 31 August 1796 and limestone from the quarries near Doveholes was transported into Marple. Samuel Oldknow's limekilns were now operational and coal and limestone were shipped to the kilns along two arms that lead from Marple Basin, while lime and lime ash were loaded on the short arm which ran from Posset Bridge in central Marple.

Despite the opening of the 'upper' canal, the company was still short of funds. In March 1797 work was stopped on the 'lower' canal while the committee arranged for a new issue. Even with this there was still insufficient money available and it was decided not to build the proposed flight of sixteen locks at Marple but to install a single-track tramroad instead. The company also tried to encourage trade by reducing toll rates on lime, limestone, building stone and coal destined for limekilns. With the tramroad replacing the locks, the canal, including the Whaley Bridge branch, was open for traffic on 1 May 1800. The work to that point had cost £117,140, £36,540 of which had been borrowed. An Act in June then allowed the company to raise further funds (to a total of £150,000) by new shares or promissory notes. This allowed the company to build an 84 acre reservoir at Chapel-en-le-Frith (a second reservoir, Toddbrook, was built at Whaley Bridge in the 1830s).

With the canal now fully operational, the problems in having to tranship lime and limestone on to the Marple tramway and back off again were beginning to cause congestion. Some 1,000 tons of limestone a day were being handled and night working was introduced in December 1800. The situation was only partially resolved when the tramway line was doubled. As a consequence, in 1801 the company sought to raise the necessary funds to build the locks they had originally planned. In August 1803 Richard Arkwright (presumably at Samuel Oldknow's request) agreed to loan the company £24,000 (he was repaid in 1813) and Thomas Brown was engaged to engineer the work. The locks were opened in October 1804 at a cost of about £27,000. The tramroad, however, wasn't closed until

Ice breakers at work on the canal near Romiley in *c.* 1903

Ware/The Boat Museum Archive

February 1807 which may suggest just how busy things were. The company funded this work through a further share issue authorized by the passage of an Act in 1805. This brought the final cost to £177,000.

The Peak Forest company now set about increasing its lime and limestone business. Drawbacks on limestone and coal were offered to investors who built kilns on the Peak Forest or neighbouring canals. They even offered to financially assist the construction of new kilns if Peak Forest limestone was used exclusively in them. Premiums and loans were offered for boats built before a certain date on the upper level. Special promotions of Peak Forest limestone were made to sites along the Bridgewater Canal, the Leeds & Liverpool Canal, the Huddersfield Canal and the summit levels of the Rochdale and the Manchester, Bury & Bolton Canals. They bought additional quarries, rented kilns (which they operated themselves) and maintained a wharf in Manchester from where limestone was sold for road-building. They drew up agreements with the new Liverpool & Manchester Railway; granting drawbacks on stone moved by canal to Manchester and then transhipped on to rail for sales elsewhere. This vigorous promotion was highly successful and the trade in limestone and lime was a busy one. In 1808, 50,000 tons of limestone were moved from Bugsworth and in 1811 a maiden dividend of £2 per share was paid. By 1824 the company loaded 291 narrow boats in just four weeks and in 1833 it was carrying an average of

1,743 tons on 279 boats every week. Furthermore, the prospects for growth were good especially as the much discussed Macclesfield Canal (which would link the Peak Forest with the Trent & Mersey and provide a shorter route from the Potteries to Manchester) now looked like becoming a reality (it was finally opened in 1831). In addition, the Cromford & High Peak Railway, which would connect the Peak Forest with the Cromford Canal, was about to be built. This latter line, which also opened in 1831, offered the potential for a short cut between Manchester and the East Midlands and possibly even to London. Thus by the 1830s the canal company was in good shape. In 1832 the dividend was up to £3 10s. By 1833 it was £4 and by 1835, £5. In 1838 the canal carried 442,253 tons of cargo and the total revenue, which includes the company's own lime amd limestone business, was £19,169.

Inevitably by the late 1830s railway competition was beginning to raise its head. In 1838, the through line from Manchester to London was open and the first rounds of toll cutting began. Competition was also developing between the canal companies for traffic from Manchester to Sheffield, Manchester to Cromford and Manchester to Nottingham. The Peak Forest company supported the Cromford & High Peak Railway route to the East Midlands and reduced both its toll and its wharfage charges in order to maintain and encourage traffic. However, by April 1843 the company was beginning to feel the affects of competition for its lime trade and was forced to increase the drawbacks offered.

These aggressive actions meant that by 1844 traffic levels had increased but there was no concomitant increase in receipts. Dividends were reduced to £3 and the writing was firmly written on the canalside wall. In 1845 the Sheffield, Ashton-under-Lyne & Manchester Railway offered to take over the canal and its debts on a perpetual lease for £9,325 p.a. (equivalent to a guaranteed dividend of 5 per cent per share after the payment of loan interest). This deal was completed on 25 March 1846 and the canal passed into railway control on 27 July. At the same time, the SA&MR (which was soon renamed the Manchester, Sheffield & Lincolnshire Railway) also leased the Ashton and Macclesfield Canals.

With the transfer of ownership the canal began to lose trade. In 1838 the canal carried 442,253 tons. In 1848 this had dropped to 343,549 tons, and by 1855 it was down to 187,189. Traffic stayed at this level into the 1860s. These figures, however, mask the significant loss of income that resulted from the ever-falling toll rates. Such reductions were needed even more when the Stockport, Disley & Whaley Bridge Railway was opened to the Cromford & High Peak in June 1857. Any tentative agreements with this new company on competition must have disappeared when it was absorbed by the London & North Western Railway in 1866.

In 1883 the Peak Forest company was officially dissolved and all its interests incorporated into the railway company, which in 1897 became the

Great Central Railway. By then traffic along the canal had declined significantly, carrying just 136,148 tons in 1905 to yield revenue of £4,138. There was thus an operating loss of £976. Cargo at this time included lime and limestone, coal, stone, cotton and grain. Activity at Bugsworth Basin came to a halt in 1922 and the tramroad line was abandoned in 1925. With the basin shut, trade along the upper level of the canal virtually ceased. On the rest of the line some through traffic continued to and from the Macclesfield Canal, and a small amount of coal and raw materials was shipped towards Manchester and the Ashton Canal. Most of the traffic, however, was short haul with cargo comprising of coal, timber, cotton, shale, soda ash and acid. Olive Bowyer reports that most of the boats that remained in the 1930s were still horse-drawn although some were actually man-powered with the ropes either tied around the puller's waist or slung over his shoulder.

Through the Second World War low levels of traffic continued on both the Ashton and the Peak Forest Canals but, once the war was over, the business collapsed. With nationalization in 1948 little or no maintenance work was undertaken and it was evident that the Ministry of Transport saw no future for its Peak Forest line. The top pound and its link with the

Bugsworth Basin after traffic from the quarries had ceased, *c.* 1930

Ware/The Boat Museum Archive

Macclesfield could be kept open for pleasure boats but all commercial traffic along the canal ceased in 1958. In the long, cold winter of 1961–2, Marple Aqueduct was badly damaged when the water that had seeped into the stonework froze and caused the masonry to be damaged. Stop planks were inserted and there was a grave danger that the whole line would be lost forever. The estimate for repairing the structure was £35,000 compared with one of just £28,000 to demolish it and carry the water across the valley by pipe.

It was at this juncture that the town clerk of Bredbury and Romiley council called a meeting of local authorities and interested parties to discuss the situation. It was agreed that the extra money must be found, that the aqueduct should be listed as an ancient monument and that it carry a fully navigable waterway and not a rubbish tip. Despite these fine words, the situation cannot have been helped when further damage during the following winter increased the estimated cost of the repairs. On top of this, the sixteen Marple Locks, which hadn't been used for some time, were beginning to disintegrate.

In 1964 the Peak Forest Canal Society was formed with the aim of restoring the canal. At first British Waterways was unwilling to let the society's members work on the line. However, volunteers appear to have replaced broken lock beams and to have mended sluices, and by 1968 the restoration of both the Peak Forest and the Ashton Canals was in full swing. The passage of the Transport Act was then a great help to the cause. BW was gradually convinced of the efficacy of the project and, thanks to the Act, it was allowed to work with interested parties to further the redevelopment of waterways under its jurisdiction. Thus, with the help of the society and the local authorities, it was agreed that the canal would be restored. With the considerable assistance of numerous volunteer navvies, the restoration work was completed in March 1974 and the line was officially reopened on 13 May. Today the canal is a justifiably popular part of the Cheshire Ring.

The Walk

Start:	Newtown (OS ref: SJ 995847)
Finish:	Whaley Bridge (OS ref: SK 013816)
Distance:	4^1/$_2$ miles/7 km
Maps:	OS Landranger 109 (Manchester) and 110 (Sheffield & Huddersfield)
Outward:	Train from Whaley Bridge to Newtown (enquiries: (061) 480 4482)
Car park:	At Whaley Bridge station
Public transport:	British Rail Whaley Bridge

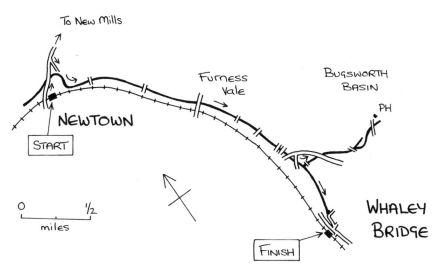

The Peak Forest Canal

From Newtown station turn left towards New Mills. After 250 yd the road goes over the canal at Thornsett Road Bridge. Although there is no immediate access to the towpath, you get fine views of the mills to either side of the bridge. To the left (towards Marple) is the Albion Mill (left) and Brunswick Mill (right). Both were cotton mills that used the canal for supplies of coal as well as for delivering raw materials and taking away finished product. To the right (towards Whaley Bridge) is the, now closed, Canal Foundry (left) and, another cotton mill, Warksmoor Mill (right). To reach the towpath continue along the road and turn right in to Victoria Street (a signpost for the canal points the way). This reaches the PFC opposite New Mills Marina.

Turn left to walk along the left-hand bank with the Goyt Valley falling away to a fine railway viaduct which carries the Manchester to Sheffield railway. At one time there were further cotton mills along the towpath side of the canal just here. One, the Victoria Mill, was destroyed by fire in 1986. The other, Woodside Mill, suffered a similar fate in 1961. The outbuildings of both are now occupied by small businesses. The canal bends right and then left to pass a small summer-house on the right bank with a well-tended garden and then on under Bankend Bridge. We now walk through a narrow wooded section which leads to Mellor's or Carr Swing Bridge. This whole section feels so remote that it's hard to believe that the line once saw forty boats of limestone a day chundering down the line towards Marple and, presumably, forty boats a day returning to Bugsworth Basin.

After passing Furness Vale Marina (and dry-dock) and a small row of terrace cottages (built for local mill workers), the canal goes under Furness

Bridge. A couple of hundred yards after the bridge, on the far bank, was once the site of a stone wharf which received its stone via a tramway from Yeardsley Quarries. The tramway passed through a tunnel under both the A6 and the railway. From here the canal passes under a lift bridge and a footbridge with the sewage works to left. This is the wonderfully named Bongs Bank Bridge. The next bridge is number 33, Greensdeep Bridge.

Walk on to pass a roller mechanism (used in times of maintenance to drain the canal by winding up a chain attached to a plug in the bottom of the canal), some houses to the right to reach a metal footbridge, Bothomes Hall Lift-Up Bridge, then a major road bridge. This is Bridgemont. If you cross the footbridge you can reach the Dog and Partridge pub.

Continue under the next major road bridge to reach the junction with the Buxworth arm. Our route to Whaley Bridge bends right here but before continuing take a short diversion along what was once the main line by turning left to walk along the left-hand bank. The Buxworth arm was opened in August 1796 and effectively abandoned in 1927. It was left to nature until the 1960s when the Inland Waterways Protection Society cleared the channel and restored it for navigation. Start by going under the footbridge, over the River Goyt Aqueduct and under the A6(T) road bridge. Stop planks mark the end of the rewatered section and beyond here the bed of the canal becomes increasingly overgrown. In 1972 the section right up to the basin was navigable but alas no longer. We pass some small cottages (known as Teapot Row) to the left and then on to a lock with Canal House and a small outhouse just a little further on. We are now at Bugsworth Basin.

Bugsworth Basin is classified as an ancient monument and is steadily being restored by the Inland Waterways Protection Society. Here is a complex of transhipment arms and basins that were once the whole rationale behind the existence of the PFC. Limestone was delivered to the basin from the various quarries around Doveholes by means of tramways and then shipped out, either as stone or as lime, along the canal. The lock at the entrance to the basin was a gauging lock, where boats were assessed for the weight of cargo carried by their height in the water. To the left is the wharfinger's office, where all the relevant gauging details were logged. The small building a little further on was the stables.

If you walk on to the newly erected footbridge, you can get a good view of the first part of the basin. There were three canal arms. The right-hand one went on to the upper basin whereas the first two in front of us were served by tramways which have been picked out by IWPS in stone chippings. Limestone was originally moved here by cart but work started on the Peak Forest Tramway in 1795. It was opened in 1796. The main quarry tramway was 4 ft 2 in gauge and ran for 6½ miles from here via Chapel-en-le-Frith to the quarries at Doveholes with branches to other quarries. There was an 85 yd tunnel at Chapel Milton (reputedly the world's first railway tunnel)

Bugsworth Basin, 1992

and a 209 ft inclined plane at Chapel-en-le-Frith. It reached a summit level of 1,139 ft. To cope with the traffic the track, apart from in the tunnel, was doubled in 1803. The stone was shipped down the tramway in iron boxes on wagons which could carry 2–2½ tons each. At Bugsworth the containers were either lifted into the waiting boats or taken straight to limekilns which bordered the basin area. Boxes were used in order to make the transhipment from the tramroad to the canal and from the canal to the Marple tramway easier. Following the opening of the locks at Marple in 1805, use of the boxes was abandoned and wagon tipplers were installed. The trucks made their descent under the force of gravity and were hauled back up the hill by horses. Activity at Bugsworth Basin came to a halt in 1922 and the tramroad line was abandoned in 1925. With the basin shut, trade along the upper level of the canal virtually ceased.

If you walk across the whole length of the footbridge and follow the course of the tramway (keeping to the left of the low wall), you cross a bridge with a view down right to the right-hand canal arm as it moves on to the upper basin. On the far bank are the remains of a series of limekilns. Eventually the path leads round to the Navigation Inn with the upper basin to the right. The tramway to Doveholes went straight on from here, whereas that to Barron Clough quarry bore right. Return back along the tramway towards the wharfinger's house. Just before the tramway bears left over the bridge, go right down some steps to a small basin that once served another, earlier, series of limekilns. Go right under the bridge to walk alongside the canal arm and then right again under a second bridge tunnel. This path passes to the right of the site of a building that housed a stone-crushing machine and returns to the wharfinger's house.

After this brief sojourn, return to the junction with the PFC main line. Cross the small footbridge at the beginning of the arm and turn right to walk along the left-hand bank of the canal. This, the route to Whaley Bridge, was originally built as a branch line. It is about half a mile to Whaley Bridge Basin where we cross an overflow weir and follow the path round the edge of the triangular basin to the terminus building.

This was formerly an important transhipment point on to the Cromford & High Peak Railway. The C&HPR provided a route to the Cromford Canal at Lea Wood near Cromford and thus to the River Trent and the rest of the canal network. The route was originally conceived as a canal navigation. Indeed, John Rennie had carried out a preliminary survey and presented an estimate of £650,000. The line was thought by many, including the highly supportive Grand Junction Canal Company (now known as the Grand Union), to be a way of shortening the route from London to Manchester. Naturally the Trent & Mersey, whose business was most under threat, was antagonistic and it appears to have won the argument. The concept, however, stayed alive and it wasn't long before thoughts had switched to a railway. Following an Act of 2 May 1825, Josias Jessop was appointed engineer and the work began. The line, which opened on 6 July 1831, included stationary engines to haul wagons up as many as nine inclines to the more conventional railways that ran along the summit to the PFC. The line was an important route for various cargoes going north–south, including agricultural produce and even water. The company faced severe competition by the late 1840s from other railway lines but the route remained open until 1967. It is now part of a long-distance path, the High Peak Trail. If you go around the back of the terminus warehouse, you can still see the loading bays for the C&HPR as well as the point where the feeder from the nearby Toddbrook reservoir enters the canal. The first stretch of the C&HPR left the terminus building and bore left to pass what is now the car park and over the river via a girder bridge. A little further on is the site of the first of the railway's inclines.

To complete the walk from the warehouse, turn right and follow the road left. The railway station is on the right.

Further Explorations

All 14³/₄ miles of the Peak Forest towpath are open to walkers: from Portland Basin, Ashton-under-Lyne to Whaley Bridge Basin. Public transport between the two ends is awkward and towpathers wishing to walk the entire route in one day are best advised to go with a like-minded car driver for a 'two-car trick'. For those less fortunate, trains can be used if you're prepared for the outward journey to be a little time consuming and you are able to walk an extra 1¹/₂ miles. If starting at Whaley Bridge, take the train to Newtown. Leave the station and turn right. After ¹/₂ mile turn left into central New Mills. At the top of the main street, bear left to reach New Mills station from where you can take a train to Guide Bridge. Leaving this station, turn right to reach the Ashton Canal. Turn right to walk along the right-hand bank for about ³/₄ mile to Portland Basin where the PFC goes south while the Huddersfield Narrow Canal goes straight on. Turn right to walk along the right-hand bank of the PFC. If attempting the full walk, arm yourself with Olive Bowyer's excellent towpath guides (see below).

Those who prefer a bit of a mooch rather than a walk, should head for Marple where you can park in the 'shoppers' car park in the centre of the town. Return to Stockport Road and turn left to go past the cinema and the Liberal Club to reach the canal at Posset Bridge (or New Mills and Stockport Road Bridge). The bridge get its name, so the story goes, because Samuel Oldknow supplied the navvies with a locally brewed posset of ale to encourage them to build the canal to schedule. They did.

Turn right to walk up Lockside. Here, in a short, steep 200 yd, we pass four locks each with a massive side pound that seem to invade neighbouring gardens on the far side of the waterway. They were built to ensure that there was sufficient water to allow free flow along the line without draining each pound every time a lock was used. At the top of the slope we pass the fourth lock of this sequence and reach the summit pound; 518 ft above sea-level. Here on the right is the old canal toll-house. Olive Bowyer informs us that the building doubled as the paymaster's house, so this must have been a busy spot on a Friday night. It is also the spot where Denis Howell proclaimed the restored line open in 1974. Part of the rationale for the position of the toll-house here is that the nearby roving bridge marks the junction

The horse tunnel at
Posset Bridge, Marple

with the Macclesfield Canal (see Chapter 8). Looking right we can see the
former stop lock that separated the two canals and an old stone warehouse.
Looking left we see the upper Peak Forest on its way to Whaley Bridge.

We now turn round to walk back to Posset Bridge where you can either
go under the horse tunnel or the even more unusual pedestrian tunnel to the
right of it. Looking back at Posset Bridge you can see that there is a redundant arch to the left of the currently used channel. This marked the course
of the Limekiln arm which followed the Strines Road to a group of kilns
about a $1/4$ mile to the south. It was infilled some time after the Second
World War. A second canal arm left the main line here and headed left
towards a basin that was situated where the town centre car park is today.
This was the Hollins Mill arm which served the cotton mill which was
demolished in the 1950s. The canal arm was infilled at the same time.

The walk continues on to lock 12 with Memorial Park to the left. This
popular and pleasant stretch passes two more locks before reaching a fine
building to the right: Oldknow's warehouse. One interesting feature of the
building is the boat entrances on the far side that enabled covered loading

and unloading. The warehouse has been successfully converted into office space and is now called Lockside Mill. The small building to the right of the warehouse is Tollgate Cottage where tolls were collected from boats going to and from the many wharves between here and Posset Bridge.

The towpath changes sides at Station Road or Brabbins Change Bridge. Before crossing, however, it's worth noting the roller which still remains here to protect the stonework from towrope abrasion. Continue along the right-hand bank and past the next series of locks (Nos 1–8). There are sixteen altogether in the Marple flight and they raise the level of the canal 209 ft. Thus, each is about 14 ft deep compared with an average of just 7 ft on most canals. After passing Bottom Lock House we reach the end of the flight and a broad expanse of water that was, before the completion of the locks, the southern terminus of the lower canal. Loads of limestone were transhipped from here to the tramway that once ran up the hill on to waiting narrow boats. The tramway took a route to the west of the current line (i.e. to the left as we are presently walking) and then across the canal at lock 10 just above Oldknow's warehouse. The upper terminus was at a point just beyond the Macclesfield Junction.

The towpath again changes sides and we now walk under a railway viaduct and on to the most famous engineering feature on the PFC, the Marple (or Goyt) Aqueduct. This takes the canal over the River Goyt, some 97 ft below, by three arches. In designing the aqueduct, Outram copied the ideas of a Welsh bridge builder, William Edwards, by perforating the shoulders of the arches with hollow cylinders or roundels thereby reducing the weight of the whole structure. The aqueduct was opened in 1800 having taken seven years to build. The neighbouring railway viaduct, which overlooks the whole scene, was opened sixty-five years later. If you cross the aqueduct and turn left down a signposted path, you can reach its base. It's a densely wooded spot and wonderfully emotive. The view of the aqueduct, however, is obscured in summer by the overhanging foliage and some may view the steep climb back up the valley as somewhat unnecessary.

To complete the walk, return along the towpath to Posset Bridge and turn right to reach the town centre.

Further Information

The Peak Forest Canal Society is presently not operational. Enthusiasts for this wonderful line should therefore seek comfort in the arms of the Inland Waterways Association which has a Manchester group. The address of the head office in London can be found in the appendix.

Information about the canal can be obtained from the New Mills Heritage Centre, Rock Mill Lane, New Mills, Derbyshire. The centre sells various books on the line including those published by The New Mills Local History Society. Most pertinently, these include three by Olive Bowyer:

The Peak Forest Canal: Lower Level Towpath Guide;
The Peak Forest Canal: Upper Level Towpath Guide;
The Peak Forest Canal: Its Construction & Later Development.

Alternatively, the history of the PFC can be traced in:

Hadfield, C. and Biddle, G., *The Canals of North West England,* Vols. I and II. David & Charles, 1970.

Those interested in the Bugsworth Basin and tramway will find the following of interest:

Ripley, D., *The Peak Forest Tramway (including the Peak Forest Canal).* Oakwood Press, 1968.

10
THE RIPON CANAL

Ripon

Introduction

The fine city of Ripon is the most northerly point on the English waterways network. As you stand admiring the cathedral in a city well to the north of York and Harrogate, it is almost inconceivable that it was once possible to navigate inland all the way from here to London or Bristol. And for most of the distance, you still can.

The Ripon Canal is just 2¼ miles long. From Bondgate Green Basin, almost literally in the shadow of Ripon Cathedral, the line heads south-east to Rhode's Field Lock. Here it takes a more southerly course through Bell Furrow's Lock and alongside Ripon racecourse to Oxclose Lock. Just a few hundred yards further and the canal ends as it enters the River Ure.

It's not very long, the Ripon Canal, but it makes for a pleasant stroll and Oxclose Lock is as peaceful a spot for a picnic as you'll find anywhere.

History

By the middle of the eighteenth century the River Ouse was a thriving navigable waterway and the people of Ripon began to see the desirability of forging a link with York, Hull and the coalfields of South Yorkshire. The idea of extending the navigation of the River Ouse via the River Ure appears to have arisen in 1766. The mayor of the city, Christopher Braithwaite, called a meeting at the York Minster Inn at which plans and estimates prepared by the engineer John Smeaton were presented. The sum of £15,000 was raised by public subscription and a petition to Parliament was made in early 1767. The necessary Act received Royal Assent on 15 April.

The Act enabled making part of the River Ure navigable from its junction with the River Swale upwards past Boroughbridge to Oxclose, with a cut to Ripon. There were to be two locks (Milby, below Boroughbridge, and Westwick) on the river section, an entrance lock to the canal at Oxclose, and two others at Ripon. This route was marginally different to that originally discussed. The 1766 Ripon Canal line left the Ure at Westwick Lock. Pat Jones suggests that this may well have been seen as a way of avoiding conflict with the owners of Newby Hall. In the event it seems likely that there was no objection and so the river was used to Oxclose. The canal was designed to take Yorkshire keels measuring 58 ft by 14 ft 6 in. Smeaton's estimate for the entire route from Linton-on-Ouse into Ripon was £10,843 11s. plus the cost of the land.

Commissioners were appointed and empowered to borrow whatever money was necessary. The line seems finally to have been surveyed by the young William Jessop under Smeaton's supervision. Once John Smith was appointed resident engineer, with Joshua Wilson of Halifax as masonry contractor, the work began. However, by this time the length of the Ure Navigation from Linton Lock to the River Swale had been ceded by an Act to the Swale Navigation who were now responsible for the construction work on that stretch.

By 31 October 1769 the Ure Navigation was open to Westwick Lock just south of Newby Hall. Cutting of the Ripon Canal itself seems to have begun early in 1770, and by 28 September 1771 all the works were complete. However, it was found that certain parts of the line had silted up and needed to be dredged before use. History seems uncertain about the first commercial passage but it seems likely that by the summer of 1773 a regular traffic was operating along the line. When completed, the navigation was 10$\frac{1}{4}$ miles from Swale Nab, including a 1,105 yd cut from Milby to Boroughbridge, one of 616 yd at Westwick, and the 2$\frac{1}{4}$ miles of canal to Ripon. The final cost was £16,400 with the Ripon Canal alone costing approximately £6,000. The commissioners raised the additional funds by calls on shares and by giving landowners rent-charges on the tolls.

In February 1773 three firms advertised that they were starting a two-boats-a-week service from Ripon to York. In 1777 a new service through from Hull to Boroughbridge was announced. By 1781 warehouses were available at both Boroughbridge and Ripon. Although the main canal business was in coal, the navigation to Boroughbridge also had a healthy trade in flax and timber, and Ripon was an important port for lead brought by road from the mines near Greenhow Hill west of Pateley Bridge. In 1824 it was claimed that Ripon lead was being conveyed by water to all parts of the country. The coal traffic mostly came from the area covered by the Aire & Calder Navigation. At Ripon there were at least three coal merchants in 1788, and in 1789, the A&CN bought its own wharf. Humber keels couldn't navigate beyond Boroughbridge which became a transhipment port. Trade to Knaresborough was also unloaded at Boroughbridge; it was then sent on by road. Sometimes, if water levels were low, such transhipment occurred at Swale Nab. Although well used, it is evident that movement along the navigation could be desperately slow. In December 1785 coal boats from Selby took sixteen days for the return journey to Ripon. The tolls charged were 1s. per ton per mile for merchandise, including lead, against the authorized 3s. By the second decade of the nineteenth century the management and condition of the canal had both fallen into disarray. The commissioners were in debt to the tune of £16,400, and there was no one left alive legally qualified to act as a commissioner. Despite this, trade along the line was doing well and there was a widespread call for improvements together with the construction of additional wharves and warehouses. In October 1819 the Mayor and Corporation of Ripon asked Parliament for authority to form The Company of Proprietors of the River Ure Navigation to Ripon. With subscriptions of £3,033 they obtained an Act in June 1820. The new company was empowered to raise £34,000 in 200 shares and £3,400 more if necessary through loans. The bulk of the new shares was reserved for creditors, who were given the choice to either accept them or keep their securities.

Bondgate Basin before 1900

Yorkshire Image/College of Ripon and York St John

The company immediately set about upgrading the line, including spending £2,730 on new warehouse facilities at Milby and Ripon Basin. The improvements were much welcomed and by 1837 Keddy & Co.'s, William Scatchard's and the 'Ripon Fly Boats' all worked to and from the city basin. By the end of the 1840s vessels carrying 70 tons and drawing 4 ft 6 in were reaching Ripon.

The Great North of England Railway from Darlington to York was enabled by an Act of 1837 and opened in 1841. The branch line which passed from the GNER at Thirsk via Ripon to Leeds was authorized in July 1845. The main line had already taken a good deal of the coal traffic to Boroughbridge and Ripon but the branch could finish the canal traffic for good. At the time, more than 26,000 tons of coal p.a. were being imported from the A&CN with three boats a week reaching Ripon Basin. The average Ure and Ripon tolls for the ten preceeding years had been £2,013 with expenses at £1,127, giving a net average profit of £886 p.a.

It appears that with the suggestion of the branch, the owners of the navigation promptly sought to sell the concern to the new railway company. The Leeds & Thirsk (later the Leeds Northern) Railway thereby agreed to purchase the Ure Navigation and the Ripon Canal in 1844. The railway's shareholders confirmed their support in January 1845. When the company sought its Act, there was little or no opposition, and in January 1846 the sale was confirmed at £34,577. Transfer took place on 1 July 1847, £16,297 being paid in cash, the rest in railway shares. The Ure & Ripon Company was then dissolved.

The railway Act compelled the new owners to keep the canal and navigation in good repair. However, with the completion of the railway to Leeds on 9 July 1849 and the opening of the York & Newcastle Railway's branch from Pilmoor to Boroughbridge on 17 June 1847, the minerals traffic was lost to rail despite a cut in canal tolls. Canal-borne A&CN coal also suffered from competition with pits from the south Durham area. In 1854 the Leeds Northern became part of the North Eastern Railway which, rather like its southern counterparts the Great Western, regarded canals as an out-of-date nuisance. The company reduced its dredging or maintenance operations to a minimum. By 1857 boat owners of Ripon–Hull craft were complaining that the navigation had not been dredged for some time with the effect that vessels were unable to pass along the route fully laden. Trade recovered slightly in the 1860s with twenty boats working the Boroughbridge coal business. Linton Lock records show that 18,000 tons of coal p.a. were moved up the line between 1854 and 1864. Coal traffic from the A&CN, however, which in the 1840s had exceeded 26,000 tons p.a., was down to 10,956 tons in 1871 and to just 1,922 tons in 1891.

By 1892 only 5,000 tons were being carried on the navigation, with a revenue of £161 against a maintenance bill of £683. Most of this traffic was wheat and coal to Boroughbridge Mill. By now there was no traffic on the Ripon Canal, which had gradually become disused; a situation exacerbated by high tolls and lack of dredging. In 1894 the NER tried to abandon the canal but had to drop the proposal after strong opposition from local people who saw the survival of the canal as a way of keeping down railway rates. Unable to close the line, the company offered the navigation as a gift to York Corporation, who declined it. The then President of the Board of Trade, A.J. Mundella, reiterated in a public enquiry in 1894 that the navigation must be kept open and must be well maintained 'for the use of all persons desirous of using the same, without any hindrance, interruption or delay'. The NER was presumably not pleased with the outcome of the enquiry and sought by all means to prevent the line being used above Boroughbridge. In 1898, 9,001 tons of cargo were carried, yielding receipts of £178. By 1905 these levels had fallen to 3,409 tons and £71 respectively. The main business at the time was in gravel, flour and sand. In June 1906 the Royal Commission reported that it was impossible to reach Ripon and that lock-gates were in a severe state of disrepair.

About 1929 Blundy, Clark & Co. Ltd, a sand and gravel merchant operating from above Milby Lock, brought an action against the London &

The former Navigation Bridge as photographed in the early twentieth century
Yorkshire Image/College of Ripon and York St John

North Eastern Railway (into which the NER had been absorbed in 1923) alleging neglect. They claimed that there was insufficient water in the navigation to allow them to move full loads and that Milby Lock had been closed for repairs unnecessarily. The case was won and the LNER was forced to pay £2,362 compensation.

The year 1931 saw a turn in the canal's fortunes. The Ripon Motor Boat Club was formed and pleasure craft started to use the navigation. The actions of these early pioneers compelled the LNER to dredge the lower reaches of the canal and to undertake repairs on both Oxclose and Bell Furrow's Locks. Although Oxclose Lock was a constant source of annoyance to boat owners, the cut became a popular winter haven for club craft and the lock was maintained using club funds. Somehow the club was also able to persuade the Royal Engineers to dredge the stretch from Renton's Bridge to the club's slipway near Nicholson's Bridge as part of an exercise.

In 1948 the canal and the Ure Navigation was nationalized (at this time it was called the Ripon & Boroughbridge Canal). In 1955 the British Transport Commission proposed to abandon the upper section of the canal to Ripon. Although at one time it was thought possible that the Motor Boat Club might take over the line, it was abandoned on the basis that there were insufficient commercial prospects to justify its retention for navigation. Rhode's Field and Bell Furrow's Locks were cascaded and Navigation Bridge culverted (in 1958). The Board of Survey for the British Transport Commission thought kindlier of the Ure Navigation, which it decided should be retained. An agreement between the BTC and the Motor Boat Club was then made in which the club (operating as Ripon Canal Company Ltd) would lease the Oxclose cut while the BTC would maintain the lock. This general situation was confirmed by the Transport Act of 1968 when the Ure was deemed suitable for development as a cruiseway. This allowed Oxclose Lock and the open section of the line to be maintained. In 1968 the club's lease of the cut expired and administration was taken over by British Waterways. In 1972 there was still some commercial traffic on the Ure Navigation in sand and gravel from above Milby Lock, as well as pleasure craft to Oxclose Lock, the limit of navigation. This situation continued until 1983 when the Ripon Canal Society was formed. The aim of the new RCS was to restore the derelict sections to navigability and to preserve any remaining features of historical interest. Society members cleared much of the accumulated debris and a Manpower Services Commission grant enabled British Waterways to restore both of the upper locks. These were reopened in 1986. Since then the society has continued to press for the full restoration of the line to Ripon Basin and it is hoped that schemes to do so will shortly be in place.

The Walk

Start and finish:	Ripon (OS ref: SE 315708)
Distance:	5 miles/8 km
Map:	OS Landranger 99 (Northallerton & Ripon)
Car park:	Signposted near cathedral
Public transport:	United and Harrogate & District buses nos. 36, 36A and X36 connect Ripon with Leeds and Harrogate BR (enquiries: (0325) 468771)

From the cathedral front, turn right to go down Bedern Bank to a small roundabout. Turn left to follow signs to Boroughbridge. This road is Bondgate Green and it passes over the River Skell which still feeds water into the canal. After just a few yards it's worth deviating for a short distance right into Canal Road. This passes the Navigation Inn and enters the area of Ripon Basin. This is the most northerly point on the English canal network! Here are a collection of buildings that include a derelict wharfinger's house and a number of warehouses with red-tiled roofs. In former times the large walled area housed a substantial wharf where coal was unloaded and stacked

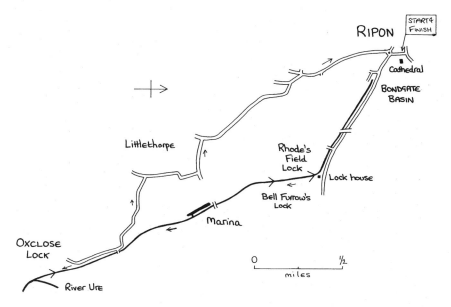

The Ripon Canal

ready for distribution. No boats have navigated the entire length of the canal since 15 May 1937 (when a flotilla turned up to celebrate the coronation of King George VI), and it's a sadly neglected spot now. The owner of the canal head has had plans drawn up with a grant from English Heritage and intends to start by restoring the cottage at the basin.

As it's not possible to cross the canal at the basin, return to Bondgate Green and turn right to start the walk along the left-hand bank with the Boroughbridge Road to left. Although we are walking alongside a busy road with industrial works to either side, the stretch along here is not unpleasant. The canal is overhung by trees, and groups of ducks stare listlessly at the passing towpather. Ripon Basin is presently not accessible to canal-borne traffic and you will shortly see why. Two pipes cross the waterway at a level low enough to preclude shipping.

The Leeds & Thirsk Railway viaduct dates from 1848 and has been redundant since 1969. It is shortly to be restored as part of the new Ripon bypass. This may seem unimportant but at one time it looked as if the new road would add a further blockage at the northern end of the canal. A little further on, however, Littlethorpe Road Bridge does effectively seal the basin from the rest of the line. The original bridge here, Navigation Bridge, was demolished in 1958. The canal is presently culverted under the road and will remain so without some not inconsiderable expenditure of cash.

Things improve shortly, for the canal bends right to pass Lock House and Rhode's Field Lock. The two upper locks along the canal were both cascaded in 1956 after the upper section of the canal was abandoned. The lock was restored and reopened in 1986; an event that was attended by a large number of interested Ripon citizens who, it is reported, viewed the occasion with great civic pride. It's just one of those little wonders of Britain that make it so hard for foreigners to understand us. Why should anyone spend all that time, money and effort restoring a lock to nowhere? It has to be said that I'm glad they did.

The walk continues along a fine straight section that improves step by step as we move away from the main road. Shortly we reach the second lock, Bell Furrow's, which was cascaded and restored at the same time as Rhode's Field. Those who own the same, rather old, copy of Nicholson's *Guides to the Waterways* as I do, will note that this lock was once known as Littlethorpe Lock and was, until 1986, the end of the navigation. From here we pass a small wooden jetty and a bridge (Nicholson's Bridge). On the far side of the bridge is Ripon Motor Boat Club's Littlethorpe Marina. The club has been the prime mover in the maintenance and restoration of the canal and are owed a huge debt of gratitude for their efforts. Formed in October 1931 and, apparently, the oldest inland cruising club in the north, it is widely recognized that without their presence, their campaigning and physical labour, the canal and the river down to Linton Lock (see below) would be mostly derelict and unnavigable.

The newly restored Rhode's Field Lock

The walk continues into ever quieter country with the gallops of Ripon racecourse just the other side of the hedge. This stretch of the canal was not built by one team of navvies but by two. One worked from the north (Bell Furrow's Lock down) and the other from the south. When the two gangs met each other, they discovered that the levelling had been so awry that the southern pound was two feet lower than the northern. This forced Smeaton to revise his plans for Oxclose Lock, which now had to take an extra rise of two feet. This necessitated the banks of the canal to be raised and strengthened to take the strain. At the next bridge (Renton's Bridge) the towpath changes to the right-hand bank where we walk along a metalled lane. When this bears right, cross a stile and carry on along the towpath to Oxclose

The Ripon Canal wends its way south towards the River Ure

Lock. From here the final stretch of cut can be seen on its way to join the River Ure, which itself becomes the Ouse en route via York to the Humber. The Ure was made navigable under an Act of 1767 and falls by two locks before joining the Ouse at Ouse Gill Beck. The line was used by commercial vessels as far up as Boroughbridge until fairly recently. A firm dredging aggregates from nearby river beds used the navigation for transport.

To return to central Ripon, you can either retrace your tracks along the towpath or you can take a slighter shorter 'inland' route via Littlethorpe. Walk back to the metalled lane and on to the bridge. Instead of crossing the canal, continue along the lane which twists and turns before reaching a minor road at a T-junction. Turn right to follow this road through the village of Littlethorpe. At a T-junction near St Michael's Church, turn left. At the next T-junction, turn right. This is Littlethorpe Lane and it leads right into Knaresborough Road with a view to Ripon Cathedral to the right. At a crossroads, turn right and walk on to Bedern Bank. If you then walk up the short hill, you will reach the cathedral and the town centre.

Further Explorations

Although you have now walked the entire length of the Ripon Canal, the Ure Navigation makes for splendid walking and is blessed with a public right of way along much of its length. One particular place of interest nearby, albeit on the Yorkshire Ouse, is Linton Lock. (This can be found on OS Landranger 100 at ref: SE 500602.)

Park the car in a small lay-by on the northern side of Newton-on-Ouse (on the road to Linton-on-Ouse). From here walk back a short distance towards Newton and a bridge which goes over the River Kyle. Just before this, turn right to go through a gate and down some steps into the field. Follow the clear path ahead which leads to the River Ouse. Turn right with the river to the left.

The Ouse has been a navigable waterway since Roman times connecting these upper reaches (to the junction of the Ure Navigation and Ouse Gill Beck) with the city of York and then on to the River Humber and the sea. Today the lower reaches between Selby and Goole are the only commercially used sections although most of the 55 miles are used regularly by holiday cruisers. The clear path passes through some pretty countryside to go over a stile and on to cross Linton Ings Outfall. From here the path joins a driveway and passes to the right of a small caravan park. After passing through a car park we reach Linton Lock with its shop and café.

Linton Lock is one of only two on the Yorkshire Ouse, and the upstream cut bypasses the splendid looking weir that is partially hidden from view behind some trees. The lock was originally designed by John Smeaton but the resident engineer John Smith had his own ideas. In the event, Smith's lock (and dam) cost £10,400 against Smeaton's estimate of just £3,000. The lock was ready in August 1769 and the first tolls taken on the 24th. By 1962 the lock had fallen into disrepair following a long period of neglect by the perpetually impecunious commissioners and was closed. Thankfully a group of local boating enthusiasts formed the Linton Lock Supporters Club. A large number of the supporters are from the Ripon Motor Boat Club whose members are required by the rules of the club to join and subscribe to the LLSC. It is they who managed to find the £3,000 necessary to restore the lock (it was reopened in 1966) and who now support the maintenance of it. This, they hope, will not be an endless task and, apparently, suggestions of a British Waterways take-over could be in the air.

The seats outside the lock-house café make a pleasant spot to sit and contemplate the scene. After a cup of tea it's worth wandering about for a while, to see the weir and to contemplate what life was like in February 1991 when the river level reached waist height. To return to the car, simply retrace your steps back along the river.

Further Information

The Ripon Canal Society was formed in 1983 with the object of restoring the line to navigability throughout. It can be contacted at:

Mr David Reasons,
The Lock House,
Boroughbridge Road,
Ripon,
North Yorkshire.

Linton Lock fans can become supporters by contacting:

Mr David Evans,
75 Kirkby Road,
Ripon,
North Yorkshire RG4 2HH.

The Ripon Motor Boat Club has published:

Jones, P.E., *A Short History of the Ure Navigation and Guide from Ripon to Naburn*. Ripon Motor Boat Club, 1986.

However, it is now long out of print. Should you wish for further information, you should therefore refer to:

Hadfield, C., *The Canals of Yorkshire and North East England*, Vols. I and II. David & Charles, 1972.

11
THE ROCHDALE CANAL
Sowerby Bridge to Littleborough

Introduction

Those who ply the M62 between Manchester and Leeds will know the Rochdale Canal. Just on the western side of Junction 20, there it is. It doesn't go under the motorway. It doesn't go over it. Instead it ploughs straight into it; the two halves of the line firmly, and on the face of it irrevocably, separated. And this is just one of the problems for those hoping to restore this wonderful waterway.

The Rochdale Canal starts its 33 mile long cross-Pennine trek at Castlefield in Manchester, where it forms a junction with the Bridgewater Canal. The first mile and a half passes through the city to a junction with the Ashton Canal at Ducie Street, just north of Piccadilly station. From here the line heads north-east to Failsworth before turning north to Chadderton and the south-eastern fringes of Rochdale. The canal completes its ascent of the Pennines just north of Littleborough. The downhill side passes along the Calderdale valley, through Todmorden, Heptonstall and Hebden Bridge before reaching its easterly terminus at Sowerby Bridge where, at one time, the Rochdale formed a junction with the Calder & Hebble Navigation.

Although never far from 'civilization', this is a fine, airy walk all the way from Yorkshire to Lancashire. It's wonderful stuff and enough to make even the most fervent canal hater put on their walking boots.

History

Following the launch of the Leeds & Liverpool Canal on 2 July 1766, it was just six weeks before Richard Townley of Belfield, near Rochdale, called a meeting to promote a rival cross-Pennine route. The aim of those who assembled at the Union Flag Inn, Rochdale, on 19 August was to take a line from the Calder & Hebble Navigation at Sowerby Bridge to the Mersey &

Irwell Navigation or the Bridgewater Canal in Manchester. The meeting stimulated enough enthusiasm to sponsor James Brindley to undertake two surveys: one that went via Bury, which Brindley estimated to cost £102,625, and one along (approximately) the present route, estimated to cost £79,180. Peculiarly, it wasn't until 1790 that a meeting was held at Hebden Bridge to take the project further. By June 1791 a committee had been appointed, a £200,000 subscription had been raised (it's said that the first £60,000 was raised in just an hour) and John Rennie had been asked to undertake a survey for a route via Todmorden. This was to include branches to Rochdale and Oldham although the precise nature of the Manchester terminus was still a matter of great debate. The key problem that faced the promoters was the objections of the mill owners whose opposition led to the defeat of the first Rochdale Canal Bill on 21 March 1792.

This defeat did not downhearten the supporters of the plan who quickly regrouped. The second bill was significant in that the committee had come to an agreement with the Duke of Bridgewater for the Rochdale to join the Bridgewater Canal en route for Manchester. The duke had originally opposed the plan but changed his mind and agreed to it if only on the promise of a transfer fee of 3s. 8d. a ton (later reduced to 1s. 2d.). The new bill also increased reservoir capacity, for what was to be a narrow boat canal, and included a plan for a 3,000 yd long summit tunnel. Despite these alterations, the bill was again lost (albeit by just one vote) forcing the promoters to regroup once more.

The third attempt at a Rochdale Canal Bill started almost immediately with considerable effort put into mollifying the mill owners and to agreeing the availability of water. William Jessop was now engaged to resurvey the more contentious parts of the line. In his scheme, the idea of a tunnel was dropped in favour of two sets of seven locks up to a higher summit pound. Extra attention to the water supply problem was rewarded when the third bill was passed on 4 April 1794; the same day, interestingly enough, as that for the line's main rival, the Huddersfield Narrow Canal.

As planned the Rochdale Canal was to run from the Bridgewater Canal at Castlefield (where there was to be a junction lock via which the duke would receive his fee) via Failsworth, Littleborough and Hebden Bridge to join the Calder & Hebble at Sowerby Bridge. There were to be branches to Castleton and Hollinwood (later dropped). The Ashton Canal was to be allowed to form a junction with the new line at Ducie Street, Manchester. From Hull to Manchester, the Huddersfield route would be 15 miles shorter but the Rochdale promoters (rightly, as it turned out) saw the advantage of building a broad canal; one that the wide Yorkshire keels that plied the C&HN would be able to use all the way to Manchester. The Act enabled the company to raise £291,900 in shares with powers to obtain a further £100,000 should it be needed. Rather optimistically, this estimate was based on one made by Rennie for his narrow canal even though the new plan was for a broad line. With establishment of the company, William Jessop was appointed engineer with William Crosley as resident engineer.

The work began almost immediately at Sowerby Bridge, at the summit and along the section in central Manchester between the Ducie Street and Castlefield Junctions. The work seems to have gone smoothly and the canal was opened on 24 August 1798 as far as Todmorden and on 21 December to Rochdale. A slight delay had occurred on the section in central Manchester although this was probably opened during 1799. A new Act was passed in 1800 giving the company powers to raise an additional £100,000 by annuities and promissory notes and this enabled the work to continue so that by September the canal had reached Hopwood. However, by the middle of 1803, funds were again running low. The Napoleonic Wars had led to a period of sustained inflation, which meant spiralling costs and an increasing inability of shareholders to raise cash when requested. In addition, the bank had refused to advance further funds until the company had reduced its overdraft. The committee was forced to seek another Act (passed in 1804) to raise a further £70,000. This was sufficient to take the line to Ducie Street and the canal was finished on 21 December 1804.

The Rochdale Canal was opened with a good deal of celebration including the ringing of bells and the cheering of enormous crowds. The new line was 33 miles long and comprised ninety-two broad locks. The size of the locks meant that it was compatible with the Bridgewater Canal but not with the C&HN, the locks of which were too short to take Rochdale barges. Cargo heading to the north-east was therefore transhipped at Sowerby Bridge. Cargo going south in Yorkshire keels (57 ft long by 14 ft 1 in wide) could, however, go the entire way to Manchester. As a consequence, the line was an almost immediate success and simply brushed aside competition from the Huddersfield when that line opened in 1811. Indeed, of the three cross-Pennine routes, the Rochdale was always to be the most heavily used.

The canal carried coal, stone, corn and lime among a wide range of goods and there were numerous carrying companies plying the route. Pickfords, for example, operated a fly-boat service from Manchester which took twelve hours to reach Todmorden. In 1812 some 199,623 tons were shipped along the Rochdale Canal. In 1819 this figure had risen to 317,050 tons. As a comparison, the Huddersfield Narrow Canal at this time was carrying just 38,899 tons. This success enabled the Rochdale to pay its first dividend in 1811 at £1 per share. An investment programme meant that this figure could not be increased until 1821 when it rose to £4, an amount that was maintained until 1835.

In 1830 a railway was proposed from Manchester to Sowerby Bridge via Littleborough and Todmorden. The response of the Rochdale was to try to unite the various navigation companies against both this proposal and any others that may come to compete with the waterway network. A meeting of interested parties was held in London but little seems to have resulted. The company successfully opposed the railway bill and set about encouraging traffic along its line. As part of this a 1¹/₂ mile branch was opened to Heywood in April 1834. A packet-boat service, operating on Monday, Wednesday and Friday, left Rochdale at 1 p.m. and arrived in Manchester at 8 p.m. From there, cargo could be transhipped on to similar services to Liverpool, Birmingham and London. These actions, coupled with the opening of the Liverpool & Manchester Railway, increased traffic levels considerably. Trade had increased to 500,559 tons in 1829 and reached 875,436 tons in 1839 with annual receipts of £62,712 and a dividend rising to £6 per share. A further boost to trade was received in 1839 when the Manchester & Salford Junction Canal was completed to link the Rochdale with the River Irwell in Manchester. And, in a most responsible way, the company still sought to further improve its canal wherever possible.

The Manchester to Sowerby Bridge railway, renamed the Manchester & Leeds, was reborn in 1835 and this time was successfully proposed to Parliament. By July 1839 the railway was open from Manchester to Littleborough and then to Leeds on 1 March 1841. The Rochdale responded by cutting tolls. The C&HN followed suit as a way of combatting what was now a full Manchester to Hull rail route. Goods carried for the entire length were given special rates. The declining tolls had a severe affect on the value of Rochdale shares which deteriorated from £150 to £40 in two years. The railways were also feeling the pinch, and by January 1843 everybody agreed that they should be talking to each other in order to 'terminate the present injurious contest'. After a meeting in February 1843 the Rochdale increased toll rates slightly and the railway company followed suit. In fact the two companies became so close that they even agreed to act jointly against potential competition from the HNC.

In March 1843 the canal committee decided to offer the M&L a lease on the canal. This was not taken any further until 1845 when the two companies once again held discussions; this time concerning possible amalgamation, purchase or leasing. At this time, no doubt encouraged by the toll-cutting, traffic along the canal had reached its peak at 979,443 tons in 1845. In January 1846 the M&L offered the Rochdale a dividend guarantee in perpetuity of £4 per £85 and both groups of shareholders agreed the deal. Unfortunately a bill to enable this move was defeated in Parliament in 1847 following opposition from the Aire & Calder Navigation which, presumably, feared potential problems with the waterway route to Manchester should a railway company take it over. What this action did result in was an agreement between the various companies on toll rates.

It wasn't until 23 July 1855 that agreement was finally reached for four railway companies (the Leicester and Yorkshire; the Manchester, Sheffield

George Stephenson's Charleston Bridge at Hebden Bridge as sketched in 1845

Ware/The Boat Museum Archive

& Lincolnshire; the North Eastern and the London & North Western) to lease the Rochdale for twenty-one years at £37,652 p.a.; an amount suffi-cient to pay a dividend of £4 per share and yet still allow £15,000 p.a. to be spent on maintenance. Dividends during the 1840s and early 1850s had, in fact, been less than this (£2 10s. from 1848–53) with toll income standing at £25,000–£30,000 for the whole of the previous decade, despite the amount of cargo being carried remaining at 750,000–850,000 tons. Thus the shareholders must have seen the deal as a good one and were obviously eager to sign the agreement. Traffic and toll income remained at a similar level during the course of the period of the lease (i.e. until 31 August 1876) and it was extended until 1890. Such was the success of the arrangement that the canal committee had turned down an offer from the new Bridgewater Navigation Canal (from which nearly 60 per cent of the Rochdale's traffic came) of a dividend of £4 in perpetuity together with an option to buy the £85 Rochdale shares for £90.

In the late 1880s the company formed its own carrying capacity, issuing £48,000 of debentures to fund it. In 1887 it bought out several bye-traders. By 1892 the company owned fifteen steam cargo craft, thirty-eight narrow boats and fifteen short wide boats to work the C&HN. By this stage, how-ever, most of the traffic was being carried within a few miles of each end of

Horse-drawn narrow boats, breasted together, pass Clegg Hall, Milnrow, *c.* 1920
Ware/The Boat Museum Archive

the line with relatively few craft passing along the entire length. Trade remained good in the early 1900s but the First World War hit the line hard. The carrying business was closed on 9 July 1921 and trade declined rapidly. In 1922 there were only 8,335 boat passages along the canal compared with 25,130 just nine years before. This decline was even greater at the summit where 3,223 passages in 1913 was down to 639 by 1922. A virtual admission of defeat came in 1923 when a number of the company's reservoirs were sold to the Oldham and Rochdale Corporations for £396,667. Some of these funds had to be paid to the Manchester Ship Canal Company in respect of the MSC's loss of rights to take water from the Rochdale. The remaining £298,333 was used to reduce the stock issue.

The decline in traffic during the 1930s was such that the last working trips over the summit of the canal came in 1939: a ladened narrow boat reached Sowerby Bridge on 6 April and an empty boat, *May Queen*, reached Manchester on 12 June. On the 1 January 1948 the British Transport Commission took over most of the nation's waterways but did not incorporate the Rochdale, which was already considered to be semi-derelict. By 1952 an Act enabled the closure of the line from the junction with the Ashton Canal northwards. The westernmost section of 1¹/₄ miles through the city remained open although, on 29 May 1958, the last boat from Bloom Street power station passed down the canal to the Bridgewater. The remaining section between the Ashton and the Bridgewater Canals in central Manchester remained (barely) open despite an Act in 1965 which allowed it to be closed if (or perhaps when) the Ashton Canal were ever closed. David Owen records how it took twelve days to navigate the 1¹/₄ miles to the junction with the Ashton Canal in the early 1960s.

Although much effort had already been expended by canal restoration enthusiasts, sadly, by the early 1970s, the prospects for the canal were still poor. The inherent dangers of an open watery rubbish tip running through the suburbs of Manchester led the city council to infill 2¹/₂ miles of the canal from Great Ancoats Street northwards. However, by this time there was an increasing interest in leisure use. The Rochdale Canal Society was formed in the 1970s with the aim of promoting full restoration between Manchester and Sowerby Bridge. This has resulted in the formation in 1984 of the Rochdale Canal Trust Ltd with the view to raising funds for this purpose. And, slowly but surely, life is being breathed back into the old canal. The Calderdale section between Sowerby Bridge and Todmorden is now fully restored although there is presently no access to the C&HN. The Trust hopes to be able to open the full line by the early part of the twenty-first century. Full restoration will, according to an estimate in early 1991, cost £15.9 million. Yet the benefits in reopening the waterway will be substantial. We can only hope that it will be done.

The Walk

Start:	Sowerby Bridge railway station (OS ref: SE 062234)
Finish:	Littleborough railway station (OS ref: SD 938162)
Distance:	15¹/₂ miles/25 km (or shorter, see text)
Map:	OS Outdoor Leisure 21 (South Pennines)
Return:	British Rail Littleborough to Sowerby Bridge (enquiries: (0422) 364467)
Car park:	Sowerby Bridge station
Public transport:	British Rail at either end

Thanks to the proximity of the railway line, this walk can be divided into three shorter lengths. Sowerby Bridge to Hebden Bridge is approximately

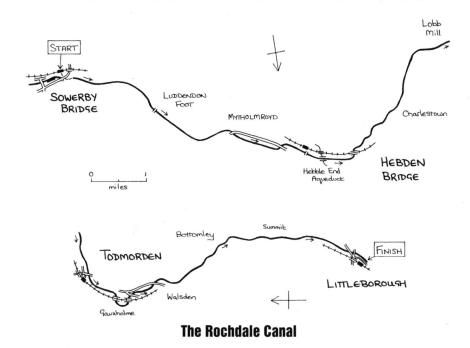

The Rochdale Canal

6 miles (9¹/₂ km), Hebden Bridge to Todmorden is 5 miles (8 km) and Todmorden to Littleborough is 6 miles (9¹/₂ km). (These figures include the distance to and from the relevant railway stations.)

Sowerby Bridge to Hebden Bridge

From the town side of Sowerby Bridge station, go down the steps to a lane. Turn left and then right along an alley, following signs to the town centre. This path crosses the River Calder with its riverside warehouses to the left. Continue along an alley between houses to the main road (Wharf Street).

Before starting the walk to Hebden Bridge, it is well worth having a look at the Sowerby Bridge Basin. To do this, turn right to walk along Wharf Street. After passing some traffic lights near a church, the road goes over the stub end of the Rochdale Canal. Turn right to walk with the rather sad look-ing Rochdale Canal to left. Our way passes two locks to reach the Sowerby Bridge Canal Basin. The basin was originally the westernmost terminus of the Calder & Hebble Navigation; a line engineered by John Smeaton and completed to Sowerby Bridge in 1774. The first warehouses were built in

The Rochdale at
Sowerby Bridge

the 1780s and over the following years more warehousing, offices and stabling were added. At its peak there were 3,673 square yd of covered warehousing and 1,800 square yd of outside storage here. When the first section of the Rochdale was opened from Sowerby in 1798, the basin became a major transhipment point for those Rochdale barges which couldn't work the C&HN short locks. The shorter (but equally wide) Yorkshire keels, however, were able to work both navigations and would not have needed to have stopped here. Some of the original basin buildings are still standing but the features are now hard to pick out. Many of the structures have large arches to enable the boats to go into the building. The last barge to use these facilities left in September 1955.

The walk continues round the towpath to reach the C&HN. Walk on to go under a bridge and up the other side to the road. Cross the canal and then return to Sowerby Bridge along the wharf side with the basin still to the left. Here we can see the new function of the basin: in part home to Shire Cruisers; in part, converted into The Moorings Bar and Restaurant.

To start the walk proper return to the station alleyway. Cross Wharf Street via the pedestrian crossing and walk into the car park opposite with the public conveniences to your right. Bear left in the car park to reach the truncated end of the Rochdale Canal which starts near the Kwiksave supermarket. To rejoin the Rochdale Canal with the C&HN will be no easy matter; the cost of doing so was estimated in early 1991 as £2.5 million. The walk starts along the left bank of the canal with a series of old canal buildings to the left. The line soon bends right and goes under a footbridge. Within a relatively short distance the canal seems to leave the town behind with the River Calder down to the left and an embankment right which appears to have been hewn out of solid rock.

Further on, we go through the 43 yd (and hence rather misnamed) Sowerby Long Tunnel, originally the only one on the canal. After the tunnel we pass a steep cliff up to the right to a suburb of Sowerby Bridge called Friendly. A large, rather tentatively perched, house (called, appropriately enough, Canal View) peers down on the canal. The river is now quite close to the left. We cross an overflow weir and pass a sewage farm. After High Royd Bridge the scene becomes much quieter. Although the river below is swathed in rubbish, the view is typical south Pennine countryside: green and lush fields separated by angular stone walls. The next bridge is Longbottom Bridge, which for a long time was culverted. It has now (since 30 September 1987) been restored by Calderdale Metropolitan Borough Council as part of the Manpower Services Commission Community Programme. The towpath has also received considerable attention in recent years under the Rochdale Canal Restoration Scheme partly paid for by the European Commission Regional Redevelopment Fund. As a result, the towpath all the way along is wide, dry and firm under foot.

We pass some mills to the left and go under a bridge to reach Luddendon Foot where a steep bank rises to the A646 to the right. After passing some large mill buildings to the right there is a picnic spot on the left and a Rochdale Canal Company post. The car park just before Station Road Bridge marks the site of the old Luddendon Foot Wharf. After the bridge the route goes over a small aqueduct which crosses the River Ludd, a tributary of the Calder. If you are thirsty, go up to the bridge and cross the main road to the Coach and Horses pub. After the next bridge the towpath goes over a weir via stepping stones and on to two locks in quick succession: Brearly Lower and Upper Locks (Nos. 5 and 6). The canal now makes a sweep to the left with a road high on the bank to the right. The next bridge is a new one and, rather unsympathetically, has no towpath so we have to go over the top. We enter Mytholmroyd by going under the A646, the bridge of which has a building on top of it. Immediately on the left just after the bridge is the White Lion pub. Shortly thereafter there is a newish road bridge followed by some industrial works.

After passing the much-restored Redacre Mill Hotel and going under a minor road bridge (note the well-worn rope marks on the sides of the arch), the canal heads back into open country and on to Broad Bottom Lock (No. 7) with an old mill building on the left. Among other things, the old mill houses Walkley Clogs; apparently the only mill in the UK still making traditional clogs using age-old methods. It is open for visitors, many of whom arrive from Hebden Bridge via Calder Valley Cruising's water bus which stops just here near a winding hole.

The second tunnel on the route is met shortly after the mill. It is not blessed with a towpath. Walkers are therefore forced to cross the road and to go down the slope behind the crash barrier. The canal continues under a bridge and on to Mayroyd Mill Lock (No. 8). By now, the outskirts of Hebden Bridge are beginning to make themselves felt and we reach bridge 128 which offers access to Hebden railway station to the left.

Hebden Bridge to Todmorden

If coming from Hebden Bridge railway station, leave the station and follow the road round over the River Calder to the canal bridge. Turn right, walk down the slope to the canal and turn left to walk along the left-hand bank and under bridge 128.

The path starts with a park to the left and the backs of a row of houses to the right. Shortly we reach central Hebden Bridge with Hebden Bridge Marina on the opposite bank. This is the base of Calder Valley Cruising which runs regular trips along the canal using both powered and horse-drawn boats (enquiries to: (0422) 844833). After going under a footbridge the towpath rises up to Blackpit Lock (No. 9). The lock itself is a bit of a split personality as it has two sets of recesses in the lock chamber walls. At one time, as a water conservation measure, it was intended to install two sets of gates so that when a short boat from the Calder & Hebble used the lock, it wasn't necessary to use the full chamber.

The towpath changes sides here but if you walk on along the left bank for a short distance, you will cross Hebble End Aqueduct which goes over the River Calder. A good view of the rather heavy, Brindley-esque, aqueduct with its four low arches, can be had by walking briefly up a path to the left. Return to Blackpit Lock and continue the walk along the right-hand bank. The route continues by crossing the aqueduct and passing a craft centre before going under a bridge at Hebble End. We now pass two locks (Stubbings Locks) and go under a minor road bridge. The river is now close to the right and when I was here it was stained a rather peculiar purple colour. To the left is a steep, thickly-wooded slope.

After going under the railway and passing the buttress of an old bridge, we walk on to Rawden Mill Lock (No. 12). The countryside is now opening out again although we are still relatively close to the main (A646) road, which is on the right. The rest is hills, trees and willow-herbs. Go under another minor road bridge, Callis Bridge where the Pennine Way crosses the canal, to Callis Lock (No. 13) and then on for what must be the closest most people would want to come to a sewage works. After an accommodation bridge and a minor road, we reach Holmcoat Lock (No. 14). We now wend our way through some peaceful country under a small road bridge and then past Calder Bank House which serves lunches and teas. After the next small road bridge, we pass Shawplains Lock (No. 15) and Lob Mill Lock (No. 16) in which the lock bridge appears to be upstream rather than down.

We reach the outskirts of Todmorden at the large, and now sadly dilapidated, Thomas Binns clogmaker mill building. This fine structure was built in 1832 and has a series of canalside loading bays. Immediately after this is Woodhouse Bridge and lock 17 which, when I was here, was doubling as a swimming pool for a large group of local kids. Factories and old mill buildings now begin to surround the line and, after a couple of small road bridges, the canal heads into the centre of Todmorden. We pass a wharf area to the right (now a car park) and then Shop Lock (No. 18). Go under the main road bridge (dated 1864) via the horse tunnel and rise up to Todmorden Lock (No. 19). If continuing here, cross the tail of the lock and walk on along the left-hand bank. For Todmorden station, turn right to reach the road and then left.

Todmorden to Littleborough

From Todmordon BR station go down the road ahead and turn right to reach a bridge over the canal near the Golden Lion pub. The walk starts along the left-hand bank at Todmorden Lock (No. 19).

The canal now bends left with a high railway embankment to the right. Go under a bridge and pass the cenotaph-like abutments of an old tramway. There are now two locks in quick succession. This is Gauxholme and in front of us is the extravagant, castellated viaduct which carries the Calderdale railway line from Todmorden to Littleborough. The canal goes under the viaduct and past the two Gauxholme Locks. Here the waterway seems to head straight towards the moorland but, in fact, it winds around some houses and under another road bridge to reach Gauxholme Upper Lock. Here is an old warehouse, now home to a building supply company, with its own canalside entrance.

Gauxholme Viaduct near Todmorden

The railway recrosses the canal, this time by a somewhat less flamboyant structure and the towpath then continues on to a new bridge which doesn't have a towpath. As the towpath changes sides here, cross both the road and the canal to continue along the right-hand bank. Walk on to the next lock, Smithholme Lock (No. 25), the gates of which were donated by the Halifax Building Society in April 1990. The canal bends right then left to Pinnel Lock (No. 26) near Walsden station. After a side weir and a small road bridge the canal bends right to another bridge and Travis Mill Lock (No. 28), with Birkshall Wharf on the left. The canal is now winding itself up to the summit and the locks are coming thick and fast. There now follows: Nip Square Lock (No. 29), Winterbutlee Lock (No. 30), White Bank Lock (No. 31), Sands Lock (No. 32), Bottomley Lock (No. 33), a lock known to me only as No. 34, Warland Lock (No. 35) and, finally, East Summit or Longlees Lock (No. 36) with its white-painted lock-keeper's cottage (Longlees).

The summit pound was just a trickle when I passed this way and the mud at the bottom was littered with miscellaneous debris including the bones of a narrow boat and a tub-boat. There is also a motley collection of bedsteads, children's toys, bicycle wheels, old wheelbarrows and, yes, the ubiquitous supermarket trolley. All this but little sign of the chemical works which once, apparently, straddled the canal here. It must have been a bleak place for a factory in winter, and it's said that boats were often frozen up for weeks on end during really harsh weather.

After about half a mile we reach a feeder from nearby Chelburn reservoir. This is shortly followed by West Summit Lock (No. 37) and the start of the descent into Manchester. The canal itself is now in water again and pretty soon we reach another lock (No. 38) with the outskirts of Littleborough to the right and a huge quarry to the left. Six locks now follow in quick succession. Some of the upper locks are so close together that the intervening pounds have been widened in order to ensure that sufficient water is available to keep the system in operation. On the way down this descent we pass the substantial Courtaulds Mill which dominates the canal. If this isn't dark and satanic then what is? While passing the mill keep an eye open to the right for a fine cast-iron aqueduct which carries a small stream over the railway line, which has just reappeared from its sojourn into the summit tunnel. There are now only three further locks before we reach Littleborough Bottom Lock (No. 48). The canal now bends right to reach a road (Canal Street) which runs parallel with the waterway. After 100 yd turn right to leave the canal and go under the railway to reach Littleborough station and bus-stops.

Further Explorations

The canal in Manchester has received considerable attention of late from the Manchester Development Corporation. It is no longer the eyesore it once was and, although some industrial archaeologists hate such restorations, it is now a fine place for a stroll of a little over 2 miles. Start from the Metrolink station at G-Mex. Walk along Liverpool Road towards the Museum of Science and Industry. When you reach the Castlefield Hotel, turn left to go down some steps to the Castlefield Basin and Potato Wharf (where, despite the name, various kinds of produce were unloaded). Continue along the left-hand bank and under a splendid series of railway viaducts which provide the passing towpather with the feeling of walking into a high cave. Continue across a new cast-iron bridge and out into the open. Now bear left across a bridge.

To the left here is the end of the Rochdale Canal and to the right is the Manchester terminus of the Bridgewater Canal. The lock is the ninety-second on the Rochdale (although it was actually built by the Bridgewater) and the start of what is known as the Rochdale Nine through central Manchester. To the left of the lock is one of the original lock-keeper's cottages, reputedly built on the skew in order to enable the keeper to look up and down the line. Just across the canal is Dukes 92, a pub-cum-wine bar which has been built in an old stable. If you look closely at the lock you'll notice that the arms of the downstream gates are so close to the bridge that they're shorter than would otherwise be expected. A chain and wheel system has been employed to help open them.

Our route goes left here along the Rochdale but, before proceeding, its worth just walking on to the right of the pub to peer over the wall towards a loop that runs towards the River Medlock. This arm, originally part of the Bridgewater Canal, turned a full half-circle to disappear into a tunnel that we shall see later. On the far wharf is the superb 1830 middle warehouse that has been converted into offices and apartments and renamed Castle Quay. The massive loading and unloading bays have been cleverly incorporated into the design of what is now a splendid looking building.

Return to Dukes 92 and turn right to start the walk. Almost immediately, the canal passes through a section that has been cut through solid sandstone. On the left are a series of derelict warehouses after which is another railway bridge. We then pass an arm that seems to disappear into a low cave. This was formerly the underground part of the Bridgewater that was mentioned earlier. It's low height is explained by the fact that the Rochdale has risen a lock's depth compared with the Bridgewater. In its operational days (which probably began in 1765), boats from the Worsley coal-mine were driven into the tunnel and under a shaft which led up to street level. Coal was loaded into a container which was hoisted upwards by a swivel crane. The container was then unloaded and returned down the shaft to the boat.

A little further on is an old coal wharf where the wooden jetties are, remarkably, still in position. After passing under Deansgate Tunnel we reach the next two locks (Nos. 90 and 91). Albion Street Bridge and then lock 89 follow. Shortly after the lock, on the opposite bank, is the site of the former Manchester & Salford Junction Canal. This short line, of about a mile, ran almost due west to link the Rochdale with the Irwell Navigation and the Manchester, Bolton & Bury Canal. It was opened in 1839 and had a 500 yd long tunnel and four locks. Although closed in the 1870s, some parts of the line are still extant. The tunnel was apparently used in the Second World War as an air-raid shelter.

The line now bends left to approach Oxford Street Bridge with a view of the Refuge Building tower and a glimpse of the Palace Theatre. We are followed under the bridge by a pipe which was formerly part of a steam-heating scheme operated by a nearby power station. The extravagant and intriguing loops that occur frequently along the way are expansion bends. On the other side of the bridge we pass lock 88 to reach Princess Street. Go up to the road and cross the canal to walk along the left bank or, more correctly, along Canal Street. We pass lock 87 and Sackville Street to reach

Chorlton Street where a lock-keeper's cottage straddles the canal. Lock 86 follows almost immediately and we recross the line at Minshull Street to resume along the towpath on the right bank. Shortly we enter into the chasm that is known as the Undercroft. The canal here passes directly under some buildings and there is even a lock buried in the cave.

We see light again at the final lock of the flight at Dale Street. Here we can see the old line of the Rochdale ahead. If you turn right to reach the road and right again, you can walk up to the former entrance to the Rochdale company's Dale Street Basin. In 1822 the company built this rather fancy gateway to their wharves and it still serves this purpose today. Sadly, however, the entrance is not to a canal basin but to the company's modern mainstay, a car park. If you peer through the gates, the canal can be seen heading west. To the right in the distance is Ducie Street Junction and the bridged entrance to the Ashton Canal, a line to both the Peak Forest and the Huddersfield Canals.

Continue along Dale Street to reach the centre of town and Manchester Victoria station. To reach Piccadilly station, return back over the canal and turn right along Ducie Street and then turn left.

Further Information

The Rochdale Canal Society is the leader in the task of reforging the cross-Pennine route via Hebden Bridge:

> The Rochdale Canal Society Ltd,
> 3 The Broad Ing,
> Passmonds,
> Rochdale,
> Lancs. OL12 7AR.

The history of the line is described within the pages of:

Hadfield, C. and Biddle, G., *The Canals of North West England*, Vols. I and II. David & Charles, 1970.
Owen, David, *Canals to Manchester*. Manchester University Press, 1977.

12
THE SANKEY BROOK NAVIGATION
Sankey Bridges to Widnes

Introduction

The accolade of being the first English canal is one that is busily fought over. The Sankey Brook Navigation, or the St Helens Canal, is, if we are absolutely correct, the first navigable waterway that was built as an artificial cut separate from a river. This differentiates it from the Fossdyke or the Exeter Canal, both of which are based on natural water courses. It would be worthy of inclusion here for that fact alone but there is far more to the Sankey than just that.

The $12^1/_2$ mile long navigation begins in central St Helens. The current terminus, near Safeways car park, is not the original. In its working days the line was about half a mile longer, running along the course of the present Canal Street. From St Helens, the canal heads north-east and then east to Newton Common on the outskirts of Newton-le-Willows. Now the line gradually bends south to go under the M62 and past the outskirts of Warrington to Sankey Bridges. Originally the canal terminated here but later additions mean that the line now turns westwards to run parallel with the Mersey for an almost straight 5 miles into Widnes. At Spike Island the canal ends with a lock down to the river for a route on to Liverpool.

It has to be said that the thought of walking between Warrington and Widnes didn't appeal very much. I put it off and put it off and it ended up as the last canal that I walked for this series of books. I was wrong! The Sankey has a lot going for it. It's not pretty but there's plenty to see and lots of, almost, fresh air.

History

In the seventeenth century the salt producers of Cheshire made the first move to use coal rather than wood to heat their salt pans. The heavy demand for coal which this switch produced was one that was difficult to meet using the then primitive road system of the area, but with the opening of the Weaver Navigation during the 1730s, coal from Lancashire was able to reach this important market. At about the same time, Liverpool was beginning to become an important port and a significant industrial centre. With its growth came another major potential market for Lancashire coal.

Although access to the coalfields around St Helens had been improved with the opening of various turnpikes into the area, in June 1754 the high level of the tolls persuaded Liverpool Council to survey the Sankey Brook from the Mersey to the coalfields of Parr and St Helens. The brook was already navigable for $1^1/4$ miles from the river to the quay at Sankey Bridges where there were a number of private wharves established by 1745. By the time of the survey there were also a group of warehouses, a coalyard and a public house. The survey was undertaken by Henry Berry, a dock engineer at Liverpool. He reported to the council that the brook could be rendered navigable and it was agreed that a bill should be sought to construct the new navigation. In an invitation to investors, the council claimed that the line would supply Liverpool with coals 'which of late years are become scarce and dear and the measure greatly lessened to the great imposition and oppression of the trades, manufacturers and inhabitants'.

The two key subscribers to the venture were John Ashton, a Liverpool merchant who owned the Dungeon salt-works, and John Blackburne, who owned salt-works in Liverpool and Northwich. Ashton took up 51 of the 120 available shares in the project. The bill was widely supported by local landowners and colliery proprietors, and was passed on 20 March 1755. The Act authorized the making navigable of the Sankey Brook and the construction of three small branches. In practice, Sankey Brook was far too small to render navigable and the new line was to be built as a canal rather than an upgraded river. This point wasn't stressed in the Act and the proprietors essentially built a canal with a navigation Act. Permission to construct any artificial cuts at all was only included as a rather bland clause which allowed them to be built where deemed (by the proprietors) to be necessary. Thus the proprietors avoided stimulating opposition from landowners which may otherwise have led to the defeat of the bill. Apart from detailing the course of the line, the Act determined a maximum toll rate of 10d. a ton with limestone, paving stones, granite, soapers waste, manures and road-building materials to be carried free. The Act also stated that the work had to be completed before 29 September 1766. There were no limits set to the company's powers to raise capital.

The work began on 5 September 1753. It appears to have gone smoothly for an advertisement in November 1757 announced that the line was operational from Sankey Lock, in Sankey Bridge, as far as Haydock and Parr collieries. There were eight single locks and a staircase pair, the Old Double Lock. The construction to this point included the north (Penny Bridge or Blackbrook) branch (5/8 mile), and the west (Gerard's Bridge) branch (1 1/2 miles). The cost so far was £18,600. By February 1758 Sankey coal was being advertised in Liverpool and a triangular trade had grown in which coal was loaded on the navigation, taken to Liverpool and unloaded. From there the goods were taken for delivery to Bank Quay. The vessels then ran empty back to the Sankey. By spring 1759 the navigation was built to Gerard's Bridge. The Blackbrook branch was probably completed by 1762 (it was extended in 1770).

It wasn't until 1772 that the canal was extended beyond the Old Double Lock past another staircase pair, the New Double Lock, to Boardman's Bridge to complete the original scheme. The extension to the St Helens terminus that we see today (and on a further 1/2 mile to the site of the Ravenhead Copper Works and St Helens Crown Glass Works) wasn't completed until later in the 1770s. As soon as the full line was open, the company set about encouraging trade, and in April 1761 toll rates were reduced to 7d. a ton. Boats that plied the line carried cargo loads of 40–8 tons, drawing up to 5 ft 4 in.

When first opened the southern terminus of the canal was a lock into the Sankey Brook at Sankey Bridges. When tides were favourable, boats passed along the brook to the Mersey. Having to rely on the tides was soon found to be inconvenient, and in 1762 the company authorized an extension of nearly 1 1/2 miles to Fiddlers Ferry where traffic could lock directly into the Mersey. Craft were charged an extra toll of 2d. for using the new cut. Fully loaded boats were still held up at neap tides for three days a month but this was far better than hitherto. The original lock was still sometimes used thereafter when the line was busy and the tides favourable.

From opening, the navigation was a success. In 1771, 89,721 tons of goods were carried along the line: 45,569 for Liverpool and 44,152 tons for Warrington, the Weaver and elsewhere. (It should be noted that a ton was measured as 63 cubic feet, the weight of which will vary according to the quality of the coal. Estimates suggest that a ton here may well mean 27–8 cwt and not 20 cwt as would be expected.) From October 1774 the canal faced competition for the Liverpool coal business from the newly opened Leeds & Liverpool Canal which ran from Wigan via the Douglas Navigation. To counter this, the SBN appointed its own coal agents in Liverpool (to prevent malpractice) and it sought lower prices. The proprietors also entered the carrying business. The moves must have been a success for the company paid its first dividend in April 1761 and by 1785 its £155 shares were valued at £300 each; suggesting dividends of £15 a share.

The SBN was also stimulating a considerable growth of industry along its route. The British Cast Plate Glass Manufacturers established a plant in St Helens in 1773. It was the first plate glass works in Britain. By 1780 the Ravenhead copper smelting works had also been built and new collieries were being opened. Coal and raw materials were now being shipped into St Helens as well as away from it and finished goods were being exported. As a consequence, the beginning of the nineteenth century saw the profitability of the SBN still increasing. Dividends between 1805 and 1816 averaged between £44 and £58 p.a. and in 1815 the volume of traffic carried was up to 181,863 tons.

Despite continuing success and dividends of 33 per cent, the proprietors seemed unwilling to develop the line and several suggestions for links with the Mersey & Irwell Navigation were rebuffed. It wasn't until the dawn of the railway age that the SBN finally moved to improve the navigation. That threat first came in October 1824 when the promoters of the Liverpool & Manchester Railway made it plain that they viewed the shipment of coal from the St Helens field to Liverpool as a major target. If this wasn't bad enough, the colliery owners themselves were actively promoting a line of their own from St Helens to a dock at Runcorn Gap, Widnes. This move resulted in an authorizing Act for the St Helens & Runcorn Gap Railway that was passed on 29 May 1830. As if to add insult, the new line was to cross the SBN twice: at Hardshaw Mill and Burtonwood.

The SBN's proprietors met the threat by extending the canal for a further 3½ miles along a line parallel with the Mersey to the Runcorn Gap where there was to be a dock and river entrance. This scheme had been originally discussed in 1819 and was intended to avoid Mersey shallows which impeded traffic at low tide. The extension was authorized by an Act in 1830 with the entrance lock at Fiddlers Ferry remaining operational until 1846. The Act enabled the company to borrow £30,000 to finance the new works which were engineered by Francis Giles and opened in July 1833. Twin locks, 79 ft by 20 ft, were built at the Mersey entrance. The 1830 Act also enabled the SBN to form a new incorporated Company of Proprietors which could issue four new £200 shares for each of the 120 old £155 shares. The nominal capital therefore became £96,000. Toll charges, however, were frozen at the original level.

The St Helens & Runcorn Gap Railway opened on 21 February 1833 and was blessed with its own dock at Widnes; reputedly the first purpose-built railway dock in the world. The SH&RGR had cost £200,000; a considerable overspend which stopped the company from building branch lines to as many collieries as it had hoped. Passenger traffic was not forthcoming

The United Alkali Co. Ltd's jigger flat *Santa Rosa* after having been launched from the Clare & Rideway's yard at Sankey Bridges in 1906

Ware/The Boat Museum Archive

and movement along the line was hindered by two inclined planes. By July 1834 the railway was only barely solvent while the canal was still flourishing. In fact the competition between the canal and the railway had stimulated a round of toll reductions and, in turn, this had increased traffic levels. In 1836 the SBN moved 170,000 tons of coal whereas the SH&RGR shipped 130,000. By 1845 the equivalent figures were 440,784 and 252,877.

Although trade was flourishing, a meeting of SH&RGR shareholders in February 1838 considered amalgamation with the SBN. The SBN agreed but the SH&RGR's financial position postponed the deal. It wasn't until January 1844 that talks were reopened and the SBN agreed to sell to the railway for £144,000 (together with the transfer of its debt of £29,450). The new company, the St Helens Canal & Railway Company was authorized by an Act passed on 21 July 1845. This Act obliged the new company to maintain the canal although, should any part of the line prove uneconomic, closure would be allowed with the agreement of the Board of Trade. At the time, the income on the canal was £21,373 p.a. with a surplus of £13,581. The most important traffic was coal with 693,000 tons being shipped from the St Helens field in 1846. Most of this was moved to Liverpool although there was still a substantial trade to the Cheshire salt-works. In 1847 the company also started to sell some of its canal water to neighbouring factories.

The future of the amalgamated company was, however, definitely with track rather than water. A series of new railway construction projects were keenly supported whereas the old canal line was essentially allowed to stay as it was. By 1853, mostly as a result of the opening of a railway line to a new Garston Dock, the company's railway tonnage exceeded that of the canal for the first time: 613,805 tons by rail against 510,668 by canal. Despite this, canal traffic continued to increase; tonnage was up 17 per cent between 1853 and 1856.

In 1860 the company leased the Warrington–Garston line to the London & North Western Railway. By 1864 the LNWR had absorbed the whole of the St Helens railway and canal and the old company was dissolved. Under the Act of 1845 powers to close parts of the canal were removed and the LNWR was committed to keeping it open to traffic, dredged and in water to a depth of 6 ft 3 in. This condition must have been aggravating to the LNWR as by this time the canal was said to have been in 'miserable order'. LNWR was forced to spend £23,000 to get it into a navigable state. The Act continued the toll exemptions of the original 1755 Act and ensured that if any locks were rebuilt they were no smaller than that at Newton Common. Canal tolls were also revised to a maximum of 8d. a ton on coal, and 10d. on other commodities.

There were more canal related problems for the LNWR in the 1870s when the line became seriously affected by chemical pollution which undermined the mortar of its lock walls. The water also occasionally overflowed into the Sankey Brook and on to nearby fields. The LNWR obtained an injunction against the polluting company but was forced to buy the meadows as the quickest way of settling compensation issues. Mining subsidence also became progressively more serious after 1877. In one case the line dropped 18 ft in a year. In 1892 the LNWR sued the coal owners for damages and only won on appeal the following year. It was then agreed that the colliery company should maintain the canal banks.

Despite the attentions of the LNWR, towards the end of the century traffic levels were beginning to decline. In 1888 the line had moved 503,970 tons, but by 1898 the level was already down to 381,863, and by 1905 it had dropped to 292,985. Tolls were dropping with similar rapidity: £6,275 (1888), £4,275 (1898) and £3,010 (1905). The most important feature of the new century traffic was the disintegration of the coal trade. The canal's cargo was now primarily alkali, soap, silicate, river sand, acid, sugar, oil, tallow, manure, copper ore, silver sand, salt and copper.

By the First World War the navigation was in terminal decline and although the SBN carried 211,167 tons of cargo in 1913, it was reported that not more than twenty boats had passed the New Double Locks to St Helens since the turn of the century. In 1919 just seven boats passed Newton Common Lock at Newton-le-Willows. By the 1920s traffic had

Newton Common Lock and the Stephenson railway viaduct from a print published in January 1831

The Boat Museum Archive

stabilized at approximately 130,000–150,000 tons p.a. with income at around £5,000–£6,000. In 1923 the LNWR was absorbed by the London, Midland & Scottish Railway and it, with the support of the St Helens Corporation, closed the, now largely unused, 5 miles of canal north of Newton Common Lock in 1931 (2¹/₈ miles of main line plus the Gerard's Bridge, Blackbrook and Boardman's Bridge branches). Bridges in St Helens were then fixed at Raven Street in 1932, at Redgate and Old Fold Double Lock in 1934 and at Pocket Nook in 1934. The main line channel itself was retained as a water feeder. Below Newton Common, diesel barges continued to work to the Sankey Sugar Company's wharf (near the railway line just south of Newton-le-Willows).

By the Second World War 94,016 tons of cargo were still being moved and the company had an income of £4,289. But by 1946 the figures were 20,638 tons and £2,558. The extant portions of the line were nationalized in 1948 although with no obvious enthusiasm. Traffic continued for a while. In 1957 about 35,000 tons a year were being carried including raw sugar to Sankey, lead to Sankey Bridge and chemicals from the Widnes area. But all traffic ceased in 1959 when bulk transport of sugar was introduced. The SBN was finally abandoned in 1963.

During the course of the 1960s and 1970s, the canal was totally neglected and much of it was infilled. Some cosmetic improvements were made in the late 1970s and early 1980s but nobody, it seems, thought the line worth protecting. However, in 1985 the Sankey Canal Restoration Society was formed with the aim of stopping the decline and eventually restoring the route for navigation. The society is encouraging local authorities to become involved and successfully persuading British Waterways not to dispose of bits of it on the quiet. St Helens Council have obviously been convinced and, with the aid of a Derelict Land Grant, have regated the New Double Locks in St Helens. Other councils are also showing interest. The society's efforts have culminated in the publication of a strategy document, *Sailing the Sankey*, which hopefully should forward the restoration of an historic waterway.

The Walk

Start:	Sankey Bridges (OS ref: SJ 585876)
Finish:	Spike Island, Widnes (OS ref: SJ 514843)
Distance:	5^1/$_2$ miles/11 km
Map:	OS Landranger 108 (Liverpool)
Outward:	North Western buses nos. T9 or T10 (enquiries: (0925) 30571)
Car park:	Central Widnes, at Spike Island or on-road at Sankey Bridges
Public transport:	British Rail Widnes

There is a bus-stop (for buses from Widnes) close to the canal on the Liverpool Road near a pub called The Sloop. The walk starts on the pub side of the road and is along the left-hand bank of the canal. The bridge here is actually quite recent, being built in 1972 to replace an old bascule bridge (a type of lifting bridge that uses counter-balancing weights to raise it) and, before that, a swing bridge. The rusting metal framework of a reserve bridge is still in position just beyond. The third of the trio of Sankey Bridges follows with the railway crossing. How a restored waterway will get past the two used bridges is uncertain. The road will need another opening bridge. Perhaps the only hope for the railway bridge is if Fiddlers Ferry power station stops using the line for coal deliveries. In its operational days the railway bridge could swing out of the way; a system that once resulted in an almost brand new locomotive crashing into the canal.

The line now turns abruptly right. Here, barely noticeable on the towpath side, is the pre-1762 route that went straight on via a lock into Sankey Brook

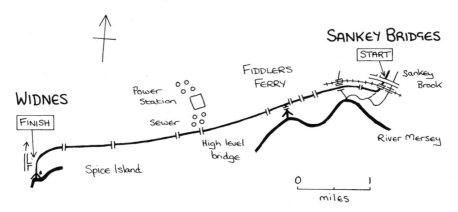

SANKEY BRIDGES

START

Sankey
Brook

FIDDLERS
FERRY

Power
Station

WIDNES

FINISH

Sewer

High level
bridge

River Mersey

Spice Island

0   1

miles

The Sankey Brook Navigation

and then the Mersey which is about a third of a mile distant. The new
1¹/₂ mile long section of canal was built to avoid having to wait for appropriate tides, making passage both easier and more convenient.

The line passes the now-fixed Mayers Swing Bridge and over Whittle
Brook before reaching Penketh Bridge and Fiddlers Ferry Swing Bridge.
The large concrete monolith on the left takes water from the Mersey and
supplies to the Fiddlers Ferry power station that now looms over the canal.
Interestingly, it is the power station's waste which is used to keep the canal
in water along this stretch. Fiddlers Ferry has become quite a spot for pleasure boats with the Ferry Inn and Fiddlers Ferry Yacht Haven. This stretch
of the canal isn't the original 1762 course as it was altered slightly when the
railway was built in 1847. After passing another swing bridge and the boatyard, the towpath crosses the upper side of the Fiddlers Ferry Lock on a
small swing bridge. From 1762 two locks here allowed vessels to pass to and
from the River Mersey which is now visible to the south. The extension of
the Sankey to Widnes was completed in 1833 but the two locks stayed in
use until 1846. One lock was removed when the line was moved as part of
the railway realignment. By the 1950s the lock had fallen into disrepair but it
has been restored and is used as a quick route to and from the Mersey.

The canal now passes the no-longer-swinging Marsh House Swing Bridge
before entering into the environs of the Powergen power station. The area
to the left, beyond the fence and not visible to towpathers, is firstly where
the waste ash is dumped and later comprises a series of settling lagoons. To
the right, the massive power station dominates everything. If this sounds
ecologically unpromising, you may wish to know that I had the highly
improbable view just here of a heron actually perched on top of the barbed
wire fence to the left. The canal is blocked along this section by a series of
obstructions, the first of which contains the pipe connecting the power

Fiddlers Ferry power station

station with the settling lagoons. Between this and the high connecting bridge, there were two swing bridges - now both missing. A little further on there has even been some infilling of the line following a suggestion that the settling lagoons were about to settle into the canal. After crossing an open sewer (which isn't as awful as it sounds), the canal starts its final stretch into Widnes. An area of scrubby marshland known as Cuerdley Marsh dominates the view to the left down to the Mersey. On the right is a series of buildings that comprise part of the Widnes chemical industry. As you would expect from a canal of the 1830s, the line is almost uncompromisingly straight with the railway line hugging the navigation to the right.

After Carter House Bridge (near Carter House signal-box), the last stretch of the canal begins. Cross the line at the small wooden footbridge (the first after the signal-box) and continue along the right-hand bank of the

Fiddlers Ferry Lock to the River Mersey

canal. The land to the left is known as Spike Island. The Countryside Commission claim that Spike Island was the birthplace of the British chemical industry. In the nineteenth century this small patch of land was home to two large chemical factories: Hutchinson's and Gossage's. The Sankey was an important factor in the development of the area and enabled transport out to the important markets not just along the Mersey but around the world. The tall tower that overlooks the island is all that remains of Gossage's soap and chemical factory and it is now used as a science museum. By the turn of the twentieth century these factories were already outdated and the area declined. Gossage's itself closed in 1932. By 1975 the area was widely viewed as a disgrace. Halton Borough Council and Cheshire County

Council then started a reclamation scheme. Just seven years later Spike Island was transformed into a popular green space; abhorred by industrial archaeologists but preferred by most.

Just beyond the information centre, the Sankey Brook Navigation comes to an end at the twin locks which take the canal down to the Mersey. Cross the lock-gates and you'll be able to investigate some of the remnants of the chemical works. There are the last earthly remains of the pyrites kilns and the bases of some acid absorption towers. The large wet-dock was once connected to the Mersey via a lock. It had been built to serve the St Helens & Runcorn Gap Railway whose wagons tippled their coal into waiting boats. From the wet-dock it is possible to wander all the way round the island and back to the canal. To complete the walk, leave Spike Island by the drive near the car park to a road junction near the Swan Inn. Turn right along Upper Mersey Road and then go right along Waterloo Road. Go under the railway bridge and straight on at the traffic lights. At a large roundabout bear right for central Widnes.

Further Explorations

Although not always visible, it is possible to walk along virtually the entire 12^1/$_2$ miles of the Sankey Brook Navigation in a great arc from St Helens to Widnes. If you wish to do this, it is well worth buying the restoration society's guide to the canal which is available from the address below.

For those with less ambition and who are merely seeking a gentle amble, make your way to the Sankey Valley Park which is off the A572 between Newton-le-Willows and St Helens. You can park near Penkford School which is on OS Landranger 108 at ref: SJ 563949. There is a SVP car park a little further along the road. From the school return to the A572 and turn left to reach the canal bridge (Penkford Road Bridge). This was originally a swing bridge but was replaced in 1935 after the canal was abandoned. Before crossing the bridge, turn left to walk along the course of the SBN.

Pretty soon the canal line is obliterated but the clear path meanders around what remains of the infilled bed. Just after the aforementioned car park, avoid the obvious lane that bears right towards Sankey Brook and instead keep to the slightly higher ground to the left. Near here was Newton Common Lock although I'm unable to say precisely where. Interestingly, the canal restoration society reports that beneath the infill the upper lock-gates are still in position. The location of Sankey Viaduct isn't so hard to ascertain. This splendid structure was built as part of Stephenson's Liverpool & Manchester Railway, the first passenger-carrying railway in the world. Work started here in January 1827 and the line was fully opened, with great ceremony, on 15 September 1830. It is said that when that first train trundled over the viaduct, a sea of faces peered up in wonder from the canal and towpath below. The viaduct rapidly became a popular scene for artists and engravers. And it is still a splendid structure worthy of anyone's photographic genius.

If you continue on under the viaduct, the path becomes progressively more rural although for a while there are some industrial workings up on the bank to the left. This was formerly the site of the Sankey Sugar Company, an important customer for the canal and, indeed the last. The final barge shipped cargo from here in 1959. A little further on, a broad flattened expanse marks the site of a winding hole where the sugar boats turned. Just beyond is a section of waterway that was restored in the 1970s and the remains of Bradley Lock with its stone walls and upstream gates still in place. Once here you can wander gently down, past the infilled Hey Lock, to a point where the restored canal disappears and the Sankey Brook crosses the line in a concrete channel. To return to the car simply about face and enjoy your second view of Stephenson's viaduct on the way back.

Further Information

The Sankey Canal Restoration Society (SCARS) was formed in 1985 with the principal aim of publicizing the canal with a view to its restoration. The society has produced a strategy document: *Sailing the Sankey – the case of restoration*. There is a strong possibility that a major programme of restoration could begin over the next couple of years. To find out more, contact:

SCARS,
c/o The Groundwork Trust,
27 Shaw Street,
St Helens WA10 1DN.

The society has published a fine towpath guide:

Greenall, C. and Keen, P.G., *The Sankey Canal.* 1991.

For historical information, however, the details are enclosed within the pages of:

Hadfield, C. and Biddle, G., *The Canals of North West England*, Vols. I and II. 1970.

APPENDICES

A: General Reading

This book can, of course, only provide you with a brief glimpse of the history and workings of the waterway network. Other authors are far more qualified than I to fill the gaps and the following reading matter may help those who wish to know more.

Magazines

There are two monthly canal magazines that are available in most newsagents: *Canal & Riverboat* and *Waterways World*. Both have canal walks columns.

Books

There is a wide range of canal books available, varying between guides for specific waterways to learned historical texts. There should be something for everyone's level of interest, taste and ability to pay. Libraries also carry a good stock of the more expensive works and are well worth a visit.

For a good introduction to canals that won't stretch the intellect, or the pocket, too far:

Smith, P.L., *Discovering Canals in Britain*. Shire Books, 1984.
Burton, A. and Platt, D., *Canal*. David & Charles, 1980.
Hadfield, C., *Waterways Sights to See*. David & Charles, 1976.
Rolt, L.T.C., *Narrow Boat*. Methuen, 1944.

This can be taken a few steps further with the more learned:

Hadfield, C., *British Canals*. David & Charles, 1984. New edition: Alan Sutton, 1993.

There are a number of books that are predominantly collections of archive photographs. Examples include:
Ware, M., *Canals and Waterways*. *History in Camera* series, Shire Books, 1987.
Ware, M., *Narrow Boats at Work*. Moorland Publishing Co., 1980.

Gladwin, D., *Building Britain's Canals*. K.A.F. Brewin Books, 1988.
Gladwin, D., *Victorian and Edwardian Canals from Photographs*. Batsford, 1976. ·

At least three companies publish boating guides:

Nicholson's *Guides to the Waterways*. Three Volumes.
Pearson's *Canal & River Companions*. Eight Volumes (so far)
Waterways World. Eight volumes (so far).

Of the three, Pearson's guides are the most useful for towpathers. However, the only one which covers any of the northern canals is:

Canal Companion: Cheshire Ring Companion. J.M. Pearson & Son, 1990.

An essential read for many will be:

Rowland, C. and Simpson, J. *The Best Waterside Pubs*. Alma Books, 1992 (a CAMRA publication).

Readers seeking further walking books should look no further than:

Quinlan, Ray, *Canal Walks: Midlands*. Alan Sutton, 1992.
Quinlan, Ray, *Canal Walks: South*. Alan Sutton, 1992.

B: Useful Addresses

British Waterways

BW are the guardians of the vast majority of the canal network and deserve our support. There are offices all over the country but their customer services department can be found at:
British Waterways,
Willow Grange,
Church Road,
Watford WD1 3QA.
Telephone: (0923) 226422

Inland Waterways Association

The IWA was the first, and is still the premier, society that campaigns for Britain's waterways. They publish a member's magazine, *Waterways*, and provide various services. There are numerous local groups which each hold meetings, outings, rallies etc. Head office is at:

Inland Waterways Association,
114 Regent's Park Road,
London NW1 8UQ.
Telephone: (071) 586 2556

Towpath Action Group

The Towpath Action Group campaigns for access to and maintenance of the towpaths of Britain and publish a regular newsletter. They are thus the natural home for all keen towpathers.

Towpath Action Group,
23 Hague Bar Road,
New Mills,
Stockport SK12 3AT.

C: Museums

A number of canal museums are springing up all over the country. The following are within reach of the area covered within this book and are wholly devoted to canals or have sections of interest:

THE CANAL MUSEUM,
Canal Street,
Nottingham.
Telephone: (0602) 598835

THE CANAL MUSEUM,
Stoke Bruerne,
Towcester,
Northamptonshire NN12 7SE.
Telephone: (0604) 862229

THE BOAT MUSEUM,
Dockyard Road,
Ellesmere Port,
Liverpool LL65 4EF.
Telephone: (051) 355 5017

INDEX

181